Introgression Latewood

Also by Peter Larkin

Enclosures
Prose Woods
Pastoral Advert
Terrain Seed Scarcity
Slights Agreeing Trees
Sprout Near Severing Close
Rings Resting The Circuit
What the Surfaces Enclave of Wang Wei
Leaves of Field *
Lessways Least Scarce Among *
Imparkments (The Surrogate Has Settled)
Give Forest Its Next Portent *
City Trappings (Housing Heath or Wood)

Wordsworth and Coleridge: Promising Losses

** Titles from Shearsman Books*

Peter Larkin

Introgression Latewood

(Shelter Partials)

Shearsman Books

First published in the United Kingdom in 2017 by
Shearsman Books
50 Westons Hill Drive
Emersons Green
BRISTOL
BS16 7DF

Shearsman Books Ltd Registered Office
30–31 St. James Place, Mangotsfield, Bristol BS16 9JB
(this address not for correspondence)

www.shearsman.com

ISBN 978-1-84861-558-8

Acknowledgements

I am grateful to the following magazines and their editors where parts of
some of these texts first appeared:
The Clearing, Plumwood Mountain, SET, Shearsman, Smallminded Books, Stride.

Enclosures was first published by Galloping Dog Press, 1983, and
Prose Woods first appeared as *The Blue Boat*, 3 (Autumn 1985)
from Moschatel Press.

I am especially grateful to Tony Frazer for publishing
a further collection of my work.

Contents

HOOKS IN CASE OF TREES

2014

some dark-green with forest Trees / The most striking, & frequent, Form of Bay, is the Hook

Samuel Taylor Coleridge

S'accroche à toutes les branches
passées et à venir, ne sachant plus
quoi saisir

Lorand Gaspar

from recursion (bough nesting branch) to a sharper
recurve of the offer   haptics at bay in broad
fastenings of tree, onshore touch bending from
norms of sift

connectivities limbed with short
(unsought) retrievals   a scarcity of
embrace proving it was given sub-
conditions at a no-fault passage   once
hooked a redundant incentive tool is
fully distributed   dry, fern-like
counter-estrangement

the contagion offers reversal of source (*ie* gift) an
on-behalf   bodied into a group of tree layered at
the rootholds of stack-in-hasp

holistic without any totals outside a cap
probing bulk offer   the pattern pleating
openly a sacral retortion   conductive
generosity is a flash of curtailment,
emergence sparks a given-from

elements of diminutive beckoning have their siblings
in leaves   to unsettle receipt signals but not the
placidity of faint arrival

not hooked *to* a
tree but improvises
inclusion in less,
additional lease
out of rarity

sheltering curbs grow more capacious than
their foreshortening, the curve
across periphery   matters of hold set to
flinging *with* the palpable, flanging a tree
of nothing but bushed curves bold to its
hook

pluck into cover bare extended grip, shake any
gouging out of grasp   these spike particles only
project as ramified

long lances of tree
stubbed to height
upwards of contention
thrown the narrows
of resort

unribbed steer, wince in the curve
a stem signal slaked of direct stress
the weft of branches round a hook astern
tempts masts to a blunter lightening,
such pendent lengthenings among lift

hooks at the tree-
purge of empty
heavens, the recurve
a direct signal
to enter preserve

existing trees to a given hook, catch segment from
obdurate crook   pose and twist a joint only
shareable hereat   snag this toward better tree

a tangent starve my centre   but stalled
(mangered) in the abating crest of
trees—trust at its lesser hold is
concomitant hook   flukes a shoot alive
in the travel silence   break its cloak of
flight across exchangeable bounds

spineless in mature tree still drawing aggregates from
hook   unadditionally the inherent cup
overfulfils its rim   an edge weak enough for lip:
scarred by tall pittances amends a frail
ontological patience becoming its "until" already in
relation   scabs early the hitch of elation

hooks in leaf
attenuate beyond
feature, soft on
futures of blunt finger

each clutch of recompense is an
immunity tallness put through
clustering   stood to the disaster though
with convergence overlooked   trans-
recession at the vertical curdle of hook

a carrying curve of leaf with dip sympathies   to
stage normative release in order to overhook it in
leaf   sidling into the reproof of tree astonish tree

I am caught by the refuels, the uptwill of
a tree's secondary hook   where root is
prior reserve not grasped as such:
what is twisted through hook is delayed

enough to filter a strategy of futures for a
minimal membrane's trap-surge:
which makes the sole relational
demand on feature

if trees do curve
are they cowering
stretched bundles of
ground in a weak
snake of uptake?

load-bearing curls
brittle enough for a
salience of unlatched hooks?

severally but at spikes of
cadence   no hooks to a
retinue but globes community
on the recurve—as ridged
to dry bud

racks up only as
levelled to seam,
what leaps gives
chase pre-accented

small occasional purchases on continuance as in a
curvilinear residue   seeding the coagulant
screening onto prongs of nature

sudden jolt at boughs, how a joint moves
onto a tighter continuum   at which shift
takes to its fo'c'sle

the one neon a green glaze outlying bent   at a
purchase of branch given on   for a fleshing up

integral hook as such not a dis-member:
limbs for the catchment of lattice, bent to a sharp
release of barrier

because local notch unravels a sediment relapse
onto horizon the coagular grains are guidant,
good barrages of gift

single tree with hooks into groves of
beginning locked elementaries amal-
gamate no grid green sliding to hold-
point, the seed of it exit-acute in field
trap

traffic of hook to
leaf flicker, the
offer is slimmer
offence than any
leaving off:
leaner if numinous
bolder if curvature

unrestrained tree canopy in parallels of hook:
dazes the wider ramification, but from this
eyelet lets a whole stretch trail the blink

refusal to merge first errors stays
conjugant at the turn snags horizon's
thicket by refracting any direct cluster
of: this is to filter an admittance renewed

to be held over common leaf as a slippage
completable, tucked into pockets of fabric

hook-curvature not clusterwards but in
saturate relay of lean beaconing

terse hook but only as one curve behoving another
by foist of branch   foil-levity of attached leaf

not to impress with
outer skirl of tree
but compact its
shrill betweens
to behalves

mazes of the
youngest hook
around cold
forest, clean
unclipped juncture

sewing an addressee on trees within their
frequency, to field the lapses of viscous
spine   bruised to its hooks of relation,
not rigid over such rallies but worn onto
a whisp of retention

fossilism whose chemistry is feathering an
armature, branches put to flights of
circumference, a scantling navigates stiffness as
the straitened invocation it is   pent but unspent
in ricochet banding around trim

scarcity the sole extra emerging from
any return on the object   on behalf of
which any refusals match slight fenders

in participation   a crushed bent in
curve at its quotas of addition

nourishes a prying lameness of attachment—night
sensing its crescent at bend of day   poor
proportions of ground to hook   in which to see a
load-pin bear the toll of curve

a double hoist (lean containment) but
unsplittable at hook   a weight of
curve on abraded risk but without any
crust of detention   once this fruitless
cage infers calm seeding

keeps micro-girded
a (tool-less) readiness
for the greeter
curvature

pressed for trans-
ience, a shortage of
passage reproaches
in curve's rapture
densely confined to
stem abroad stem

hooks can't be tensioned more than a tree will
grant but radiate with buckled span these few
states of generative encumbrance

not finally hipped into tree but do sustain
an original seizure bearing a timber's
core launching spate

how a tree will go with its loading but stow an
horizon on its hooks   its post-fuel attachments,
a wafered induration

a tree seated on roots but pleated where
frayed forward by curving into hook
range

displaced a circumference of desire within a
canopy of participatory partition   faithful to the
micro-obstructions healed by not abstaining from
the jolt to/from node

plot the wave
pitching extract,
what any except-
ion of tree
is hooked towards

not marshalling
ground but given-on
by encramping
a surround

inducing compression a range of tight
branches on handle   let hang its
unconditional curvature broken out of
circle

hooks are empty methods but call their superclip
a rise into tree   public void with incoming
populations of attachment

without dividing once local implements
are complicit   partner hooks packing
out a leafage   until subsistence
witnesses a surplus of tree crown
vertical concision abridging
(pontooning) root-throw

if such thinness is hooked to ramification, what
swells is an offering in trifurcation, entire tree
rejoinery of behalves (up, down, across) or the
lightest filter of its steepness

transitional as macular husk, from brush
to planes of leaf   from planes to a
pliancy of limits for vein   forest
breadth because there are no tandem
trees

the sediment of wanting tree ripens again at its
hook   from dead coupling to two-thirds a
finished curve rimming with past oversights of
the open: across from semi-collapse but still
forwarding junctions their toe-places, holding
partial loop at its unknit circuit

considerate marring
sway the approach
dissolves assault
from either side
of the curve

where stakes are lowest
every hook a retake
least resource docks
at the anticipation

if co-excrescence, a tree's sediment will
be its own summoning, but set before all
the woodland non-singulars of decisive
post-confinement

comes of swivelling the throw, isn't without
pulse of hook   a small hip pricks
a jointless breach

unshed cycles hang on hooks: with their
swinging what there is from horizon to
be made sparer by sheltering them, at a
cost of no peelings except pieces of
attachment

to be swooped from skies onto curl of hook:
sparse but denser loop around few deliveries,
concedes branches irradiating

where do you know this woodland is, is
hook-point a delay of shock input?
once held to a consolation there are no
more hoods   other than this gap-leaf
reprieve secured at perimeter

much grapple but
no criteria until
there *can* be
inferior arrival:
peak foliage
post-ascetic
at one tallness
of gift

earth has its
stay of glistens
poached by forest
or tapering at
hook: second-best
source crops
by its maintain

failure apportioning an outside gives whole defect
latched on entrance   offer hooks to hook-alike
limbs diversifying a branch-rate of neighbours

where trees are erect hangars they hid it
in hooks, doing to woodland enclave its
tendrils of latent tie   less any loophole
of difference to branch

a set of hooks within the kernel, open pocket of
tree   each branch foible is acting its own tag:
occasionals (tree profile) lift the quota out of its
attenuation hobble

new hooks offer small-bite angle
regrouped from tangent   a de-
fragmentation of inner muscle
finding its vertical turmoil between lobes
of sediment tassel

how to pick up
surround-ground,
ply formational
fork out of
down-eye hook,
updraft core

not in boxes but hooked until a vectoral point
becomes offered, cornerable   what is profound
in the ordinaries is the prone onwardness of any
"afforded" disturbance

trees (at least spring) bounce a cap
through indirectly erect shoot   abating
(gliding) a field-crest in focus

peak entwining enough receptant of a not-
enough: abjures its insulate paradise object once
subject to the commons of horizon   though
intermediate minutiae coil round hyperbolic grist

district completion beside branch:
unmerged limbs never needed pulling *off*
hooks

a releases-repository given a through-curved tree:
accountable webs hooked to overwrap   no such
understepping from root

the hooks' boundary petition offered first
to leaf plaint   heterogeneous sentry of
tree profile

sediment won't filter out even the leanest flow:
why a woodland's incentive-hooks amply
elongate what otherwise is target-origin and so
unoffered   avoiding nothing at bay among the
hinter-frictionals of branch community

fitting to the charge of nothing yet by
clasp   what truncates earth is what
populates above ground   a slim mast
shorting from shrouds of leaf

where no tensile relata are refused
(ground/curve/horizon) let it pass through a
narrow eye   filtering-in *at* the streaming across

hooked to tree while trees broadcast
hook-in-tree, wise enough for wind-
throw subsiding at woodland door:
combinatories of particulate post-fixity

earth-up a motley support that won't topple
hybrid hooks   enjoining frail connection more
robust than capacity entwinement

like any dark range of carrier sill, easing
off its strictures of adjoinment, slimly
barred but working into wands of shade

a contour of limits at a detour of summit re-
offered   the climate of held-to-tree occasions a
weather of horizon

rift arriving
jointure, so
hooking lift:
gift promised a
moving burden

privative hook appeals primal release, a
woodland's sore-to-sore of supra
frictionals, ashore at vertical forest edge

what intersects is momentary paralysis: strident
junction at a quantum of offering   that the
opening becomes hold-bearing, thinned tree to
steer the root-gates of forest

if the disjoint is nodal, stillness finds it
tapering   sudden minority catch onto
untrapping the rest   until vertical die-
back is due ambient perimeter

supra-segmentals or hooks imbedding grafts in
veil: what gives vertical oscillation   ripples
how hooks unforsake the flow

do trees surprise a hook or will hooks
fibrillate the brushwood trees conciliate
by?

bare arrows of
support pelt
escorted leaves

the plight of
hooklessness
would be home
losing height,
flatline missing
the joinal flinch
of dedication

thornless in
hook but shank
piercing tree

EYES ON
OPEN LEAVES

2014

Only a few looks pass through the eyes
and there are others that don't pass through anywhere.

Roberto Juarroz, trans. W.S. Merwin

L'oeil:
une source qui abonde
Philippe Jaccottet

A tree in leaf is at a swivel of eye

stems rouse into leaves, brush surface with sight

they seed the shelter of being seen to see
an eye to surfaces sometime due leaf

each leaf with its lentil speeds

traits in eyes but not so envisaged
a leaf having no face but sight

foils to observation but sap of the image

a cathected surveillance given on leaf-pivot

however lamped the terror in leaf area

shelter from wind and rain trying on
its eyes, how it pries into a tree's
dissolving underhood

because an eye can't tremble before leaf
but only on it

from blister crack to a mole
brittled enough for leaf focus

leaves per plant of seeded light

very few lenses to a terrain
until burnished with leaf
not yet shedding its optical relief

leaves' eyes lightening a brush metal
foliage until sheenless around shelter

the tree-robe approaches a state of
leaf, each canopy overlap will field
its need in probing light

the say of wrinkled tube on leaves,
small distribution spots blurting
the corrugation of hue

sunlight flooding leaves until
hooded enough to be covered
in eyes

leaves by sight
crane a tree of scope

tiny spores of surface are
gaining over sheets of image

make it shelter through an eye
of least leaf open

******

To expose hingeless leaves multiply an eye
throughout visors of entire tree

internal leaf surfaces layered
between landings of light
each riser of the retraction

not a lens sanction
direct light scraping light
for its radial wrappings

refracts through littered images
assembling occlusions of tree

leaf spots granular enough
to detect what it is light
stirs into lens

long lesions gather for light
do not deny any furthers
an under-skin

no bars as such on fresh
leaf, a lens grating the midst
of its flesh before light

each tiny leaf scar appoints
its epidermal glass, its
shelter periscope

where a scar won't sink
it becomes the eye of nothing
to wilt except stalking
the leaves' grain of sight

conduct a shelter panel out of
negatives of leaf: the surface
(reversed) is left solo with eye

perfectly unpitted lumens
skimping eye-surfaces across
light: the receptor spools out
a film of shelter

the profile signature entrusting
trails of a reflector: shoot tails
of leaf but no false parcelling

each large vein is an
irregular gallery

any spot makes surfaces a
raid on eye, untwisting leaf
at the perspective of
seeing it project

as leaf veins reveal they are
members of image, not a cradled
gauze but an eye coating its belief

stamina on leaf once flattened out
across micro-pixels of crimped lamina

a simple mouth of injury secures
sight: any naked leaf is eye
trailing for a coat of tree

within-leaf variability takes its
first look: not steeped in eye
but mottled at nodes of vision

what does a leaf look to?
what can't be rediffused is
clothing main canopy once
brighted out beyond itself

the shadestation first rationed
to each eye in turn

light will pivot round a single
side of leaf to fund a template of eye:
a plate impression of block radiance
that a canopy spots what it sees

changes in leaf reflectance at an
early infestation of nature, what
clothes the visual tags?

leaf-of-view within a single
protection mass, it limit-scans
for layers of freckle reticent
enough for retina

a pustule the image retorts: at a
distillation globule balancing rude leaf
along a beam of branch

luminescence without any canopy
vacancy but the entire macro-vault
passes over filaments of leaf

deputizes the visual intercept on
half a rod of branch, a feed-forward
nervure offering cone to tree

arising as leaves out of blink of root
is to arrive at a brow of canopy

close a leaf up at the image rotation
a hard stem is fanning the panorama

focal breadth of canopy: not
so far from what leaf asked into
discrete internalisation by a
rota of claddings for radiance

collect leaf transparencies filtering
the trim of tree but only through eyes
of the outspread itself

leaves were never adult enough
to stripe against light unless
it set eyes on them

a lens canopy massing envelopes
of sight won't omit the eye-
filters prone to leaf

clumped in whorls falling from
eyes and leaving the tracking to
scars of the adsorption

a typical spot is "zonal" at
inbound blemish, light remainder-
ed rather than blotched

eyes not just shot holes but un-
sclerotic remains on fluttering leaves

image beached as far as optical
coves, a direct-lit faces up to
coats of eye, nearest scatter gives
precise hatchings for tree

functions off platelets of shelter
scatters sight but attenuates it
compounded of gratings of light

as insulation barriers they complete
the percept: lenses in minute welter of
leaf, curve to the peripheries it lit

canopy stretching as far as an eye
can wrest its reflect-scrape from
leaf: how the leaf is exit-scape of
release from main sheaf

eyes on fillets of frail extension
attached at the co-signs of a
vertical spark from trunk

a quantum of fringed sight at
thinner fetch than any bald
chamber of deep vision

******

Leaves seeing restitution on tree
assigns it billows of light

seeing through true risk (husk)
as though unrefracting staples

see out intact lumps of light
a dapple in the abstract unless
the gaze will reconnoitre
ripples across each lamina

seeing bones of trees on beam
from flimsy summits of twig

seeing horizontally where the
trees' verticals are decon-
gestible at canopy

until leaves saw how they string out
the overheads of tree once immersed
in the glaze of reversionary frame

not skimmers but scalers by
light, where a lens might
collide with focus amid
length and depth of fins

the shellac screens will have
out-mustered green cloud: once
from scratch and no further
transition into sight

nothing of eyes to peel
this shelter, how they clot
accords with leaf scale

less skin of tree than a retina
above root: charged surfaces
wired from the back of depth

leaf with more initial surfaces
than a sea: the lustre is performative
thin swell wholly a current
of first shelter

heed canopy dissipation but only
after the fraction-touch of vision

nothing closer to covering tree
than a remote sensing

wholly visible from the spectrum
burning on leaf, miniature
crackle of horizon

no such sample holder for light,
green is already at work draping
the radiation: steep scopics
of the acceptance curve

how leaves aglow are sub-
amples, so positioning a
secondary scanning bed,
a tree's slighter wink at tree

in the crust of eyes find a
crystal of leaf, where the lens is
written into its own facement flaw

every leaf difficult to bear once
on screen: a visual lading among
shadows of tree avoiding tree

freckling does depristinate
and will pigment wisely enough
for eventual drop but falls the
sooner on images of eye
granulating to fine light

a seeing leaf gives redress to its
branches becoming so naked a percept

collective light conical once
held to hollows of tree, what flecks
in leaf is hem to the constellation

protects a foliage share of tall
bower on a flash-sheet
of the projection

a tree so slender in its own eyes,
each open lid still maculate as leaf

SHADE A GROUND NO SHORTER THAN TREES

2015

Life is a necessary precaution
like the shadow for the tree

Roberto Juarroz

shadows fell like hinges on erasures

Mei Mei Berssenbrugge

the sunlight has never
heard of trees

A R Ammons

I

The way origin is fields off
presentiment and holes trees   any
brilliant valves across sunlight reimburse
in suctions of shadow

occupying not all the spaces invents a stoplight
lays it out of ground   as on a beginning's own
obstacle

only obstruction recoils, inaugurates,
what was given at length with it

ground ceding origin at its tree supercession
a stack of basis whose after-profile gains
precise unhollownesses of shade

no shards but a singularity of ground in
section   this is what gives shadow erect
feedback   sprung from tree, averted
light astounds grounds for site

touching ground at its hesitance before light:
shadow is neither light-shy nor lidded over but
plays out enough gentle result to unblink finding

ground response not effaced, this is to
jettison counter-lacing   care prior to an
absence the interrupt light is assignment
of ground one foundation away from light

unravels the strife of real unconditionals, brings
the over-residues onto panels of shadow   a least
ripe with origin dressed

no shadow ahead of the grounds it
distanced   to shade is to inculcate the
obstruction   light is only an obstacle if
prevented sooner than shadow

a parity of sunlight acknowledges blockages
with which to mark down ground

upsurge not patterning own
wake, as shadow was never
guidance from erect scaffold

why shadows attentive to their ground
don't sprawl, here was only so much tree
to a source

earth is laid on by light but immediately induces
what branches over light   only these secondary
arenas driven below tree can render a before
its own to make for

foundations of bespoke priority under a
wood of the latter community of
temporal non-rivalry

waiting for transparency to curdle into shadow:
earth aglow is one tree-step from sun, as origin is
first to be given up   direct ground from
secondary stirrings of light

where sunlight blocks it through,
obstacle spindles are left over with
which to teach lift its ground

it intercedes for the sub-conflation, all original:
wide-screen shadow tempting grounds of
antecedent reparation

empty space finds its prepared seasons at
the divisions of trees, what the burdened
shadows striate, tabulate on intercaptive
ground   already locked onto preparities
of loft

beginnings go on to foliage alike, no loco-
instigation of their own   light is not a real
vertical but any relational obstacle acquaints it
that it is

shelteredness less than done terrain:
origin begins frail for how the trees
began it across them   until shadow
touched the reception plant

runners onto consecutive light can't be without
beginners   how shadows will allow this is not
simultaneous

that a pre-given might circulate the
initiative from where it didn't start, put
its consequents down on the site of
origin   as what is measured out by
other interruptions   stopping up light is
never ulterior

you launch basics in shades of the verticals it fed
any shadow is dia-emergent, declares ground
across a derivation of dome

that ground itself amid shadow posts
is pre-retrograde   it has to rise under
pervious trees to find branches
more original bars to light   secondaries
of offer rather than derivations bringing
slight origins into beginning

shadows relieve the implicate shirt of trees failing
complete layer, but as a source falls across
satiable outskirts   uncurt, swelling the less

vertical tread is that woodland
doesn't oversow, let shading
be as intensive as it will

II

Given the tallness of trees, interior
findings might spare the ground, they are
already due its repair

points of dependence don't puncture a surface but
its unshielding was left out on shadow

locatably slow from light vacuity
owning to tree   unframed but not
lacking shadow resolved on latency

hints at eaves roofed by ground, cathected at
shallow trunk   beams raise up stoppages of
beam

if a shadow were to bulge it would cull
the ground

since put to tree this
disastering but unprone
terrain, vertical shadow

what a tree's shade has
retracted is a ground overborn

trees aren't stalling in occluded light, there is no
thicket between shadows and what is found

horizontal overhang where ground didn't
overrun, how verticals pitch their
roomlessness

it is the occlusal outline which offers   a tree
panning its ground for low light is analogous to
vertical choices, ascriptive shade

to lock onto surfaces amid racks of the
vertical   circuits and clamps of ground
weightlessly shipped through shadow

shadowing, not substituting, a vertical cabinet of
retention fully struck by light   this gives
complete filtering of ground

lucency fencing itself a long ground's
horizon soil-vertical, shadow-led:
unprovoked bed *is* bed

the poise of a vertical undisguised by its flank
across light   not sunk into ground but its shade
allaying (signing) provision

no gap between primal upsurge and
weak particulars   all shadow will do is
divert to ground without bowing

what tree height doesn't have to disown it screens
(combs) back to ground

sunlight renewing seeds how they *glance*
within shadow-pods filtered from tree

until a whole horizon gasps at sedimented
permission, trees arcading light from root to roof
and then zoning it   surprised by passages free to
ground

shadows weren't a stripe reseamed by
outer lift, they overtake any tree-piercing

not a darkness but a speculation (descending
light) tapped off vertical tree risked lenient over
ascending sops of ground

branch thinned to amounting
shadows, ground upright
in its sieve of roots

trees do their shadow-
bidding only an earth's
away, joy of shaping
a stop of light for
its shape of ground

demotion of light like the face of the
earth, expressly below trees

amplitude *on* ground, that tree cladding knows no
infilling

origin is a tree-shoal
of traceable (basally
finned) shelter

shadeboard leafed in horizontal
extenuation   trees abide a kernel of
stiffer release

airy spans of ground not *through* tree but in the
shadow a spire repines

shadows won't sag
once on a phase of
ground obscured

lie out on unfurled
surfaces where
shading has no stalk

seal the shard into a stealth of light whose
any ground is a fragment accosted

ground occupied as a tree hinders white light
from applying?   but not the sunlit over an
ambient blue shade entering its own room

a glistener, much like leaves, filters a
blue base over its after-lobes of earth

curtain dislocations attract lateral event, vertical
ceiling collusions   sunlight prefers support at its
coefficient of shade

guestless to settlement in a borrowed
territory   how the branched saves its
acknowledgement   ground faintly
graded by commissions of tree

a dislocated plenitude percussed whole
join many agrounds sprung out of shadow

placed at particulates, that it shadows
from a germ of eventual scope
readvantaging its ceiling cope

little sports of obstacle
fed from where they
were not sent

as shadow becomes
basally free of
augmented tree

III

A shadow is not a mirage but here the
ground it lies on is no longer cocooned

trees are an ossuary of earth until fleshed in
shadow

no tenuous allotments of shade, trees are
steep in what they resurrect to ground

without shadow a ground could never stop itself
rising   without ground a tree could never prop
itself against the seizure of light

what casts from tree is what posts toward
origin do with origin

the guiding is in high band, stormy toward lights:
how the terrain's shinings digest a ration of
complying a pane of shadow   roots weightless
but standard buried

shadow weighs out the laps of origin,
flying the circuit of tree loosened but
chosen

what is it ground would wrest
from a shadowless tree?

settling on earth is a re-
position come to stasis
amid rising woods

light can't drip to earth but a porous shadow does
stanch the ground

a tree's posture grafted from its shade
(light tidal) schematics

what is common to the turns of origin is a circuit
which pleads from a succumbed spiral of trees

if a tree is loophole for grounds, shadow
is a frontier for its rootal internment

we merge the stark itself as if to stammer ground,
shadows don't drop but do fall to pregiven
blanks   scrape (script) of unfinished trees

groundward steerage solely as
underperforming the tree

recession to ground isn't deferral but a weak
fulfilment: scarcity become non-salient in shadow

so ground becomes own scarce source
crossing sunlight

due to a tree phase that arose from a foretaste
(shaded)   ground is already clouded by root

ground first but not before
except at: sciaphiliac
a tree's place of

what sustains is simply
earlier than middle tree
of any beginning's

shadows in secular refuge at the heart of
the tree/ground miracle   that light is
paused was preached

what remains in shadow was groundly retention
already appeased in tree   any accretion only
occurs to cease the extension

horizon appoints a shadow furniture
between tree and ground   elongation
once cast is the primal foray

sediment is the intuition how sunlight leaves tree-
exception within the tampon of shade

grounds superclosed in shadow but not
mined for root   foliage can be
hypersumptive

a shadow's allegation brings no alleviation unless
the between-trees drops amending pre-
occupationals   input of light mapped outside
own measure, a shorter-for

strict plenties of sun
planting a ground
squatting on shadow

calligraphy of givens to
surpassing, at anchor to
striate the weighing above:
barred light twists into hold

downshaft secondary brilliants hung off
span   how an earth blanches into root:
shadings bleached for receipts of ground

spruce without rafters in shadow   beech without
towering dark shingle   adjusted ground the only
claimant

low pressure under a stable surpassing,
not so much sheath as petal, not so
much granted as ground

a transcendence whose origin branches into layers
inceptant before light   barrier for an intersect,
uncut to ground but occupied with its shadow

a shady tree's afterward on a field of
passageability   what generates opens to
the difference of shelter from above
doing with less light at essential staves
of support   that ground itself is
staking itself secondary before

the numinous emerges mortal from its fields,
though it can shield with ground its traffic into
finite light   unconditionally outshadows what
finishing raises beyond submergence

a consistence arc offers its secondary
exits (from light) to exception primaries
in shade   ground is received once offset
(undertaken)   now shadows *will* cast

how ground bare enough for sustenance
must be inserted into the motives of its overtakens:
nurture across vertical intrudants wakes itself

support immunity whose every margin is
vertical   shadows a blockage acreage
resting on minute primacies vested by
the interruption   surer, but no taller,
than a tree

provenience storms out until poised at the frailest
cover   ante-web of shadow on an anti-crust of
origin   stubborn elevation of the unreinforced,
the exactly first

a slender terrain sent from shadow   that
no post should so penetrate the earth

to take abduction into shelter groundfast, spilt
weightless

among hardened shadows
not much stick from tree

if a shadow leaps it pilots
what hasn't fallen aside:
now earth ceases its stoop

SLANT GIFT,
GIVEN
SLENDER RIFT

2015

For Lissa Wolsak

God who holds our memories reft at pre-birth
I would trust, intended their restitution

Geoffrey Hill

1

More a salient
than onward shock,
poverty-emitted grasp of trees
taller than their assimilation

verticals straitened like a
stiffness combing its length
from grass not easily speared

catalyst sources are such
slender lines within prescription,
a gift to the brief of this wood

slants small by one yard, the space
brooks a proportion of origin

through rifts and no
unslack gathering, in
deep foliage rejoicing
less in cleft than
overlap quiver

slippage the sooner pledged
to rift: that any gift
is no path accuser

2

Gift: a small shell
found in the breach

failing the chink, its necessary
slightness, attachment to
a sporadic of tree

shrubs scarfed or
lightly plucked,
minor stripping
intrigues the lofts

a niche within
not yet counter-embedded,
recruiting norms, strict
hollows against bulk

the gift *to* nature,
only then does nature
offer a rift to itself

no circumstance but
sheer gift fallout, a
micro-slant from
vertical occurrence

3

Rebordering from skeletal,
temporal rift given to slight gate

this requited hollow offering void
attaches to echoes of void

pepper the hem with broad grief,
not quite wider sewing
than compactions of relief

the slant's non-collision just
perceivable or harshly
ascribable at the
abridgment of lack

it has to do with rifting it,
the supportive gift area

4

Slanted terrain is gift-
assimilable, a counter-slope
will drop on prophecy

pursed lair, district of the
diffident depth, is its
awarded, only *then* a disjunct

how obstruction bridges a
least as it budges
slender strands: twist at the
main abyss, a drape of
rift the fold between curvatures

thinly toned at shelf though
the rift is not lipped,
not yet ontologically
squat enough
for any spherical separation

short distances slowly
reclining the slant:
rift itself may have
been the more vertical

5

That gift is never rife: flew
into the jumps, few spans
ahead, initially without
clawing the apartness

levelling bides in a rift,
slim dark coding,
absent but wedded
to a closer breach.

can gift ruin the sill?
etiolate the gap
it was not gulfed by?

scarce provision ransacking
creation, one first meagre gift
so that insufficiency offers
a purely groundable

6

There is no mid-rift
other than slant-wise
instantives, misaligned
slope at a granting

ramped towards not
clearing the fault,
gifted (infilled) on both
sides but lacking
the comparison

technically no seal
without the slant principle

unscarring in gift: that a rift
opens the ground of reception

7

Meagre but no longer bare
of furrow, driven through gift
to chisel out flakes of ground

which doesn't brand the gap
but signs a scorched creation
alongside it, writes up ash

a breach flown apart from its
mode, foundational and scanty
but no *nodal* thrift:
small chantable donation

seed-veering cleft
where gift is
direct gap:
only the lit can
attenuate its ray

8

Yawned but hard at
gaping, a disconnect
furrows a pool
along the breach

not renderable
as sliding along rift,
any sleekness will be
its all at gift's

massive tree-clots with which
we don't stumble,
slender root foreshortening
its sites: feeding
at admissive length

9

An ash-tree's lean keys,
turn in the rift

given a poor aloft upward
slanted against asperity

no stint falters, a chasm
at its fruiture, sensing
gift, same in slights

10

Are not a loss of the numerous,
meagre branch driven on
gift, shipped within breach
but hews to endow

a hint given rift given
a sign of no further sample,
the simple antidote was in
letting gift compound itself

11

Hoping a navigable rift
wouldn't free itself
of marooned gift

this wasn't a slant
broken over rocks
but pallid nape at a
first of reception

any deep probes the
shadows, any sand
overspills the cranny

the thick branch erodes
a meagre, but not the
gift of gleaning it a
slender burden of trees

12

Everything alive, induce
mere glimpse, slender enough
to source a glimpse of
more than everything

incompletable, ends
with counter-expectation
unless it committed
what a slip of
finals always al-
ready began repletable

13

The radiance is very slender,
as witness the disagreements

a rift in the road lowers
the slant of light, this
is focal snick

slender least blame, turn
for rift, spheres that tilt us
our on/off reception

gift bowed forward, slightened
by its intake dedication,
sources a burden
cross departure

between here and the
giving of here, as
relational echo, a
here of it with all
separable least to sift

multi-anticipated slender
bearing, perched high
on a slant of beaching

which a wave inculcates
on crested ground, monitor
this station, comb the rift

14

At the rift a source
might stand, since we are
pressed to receive, along
a spine of creation

leaves the break wider
to admit besiegers enough
to a thin lair, a vant-
age in upper air,
vertical crevice

geologic gift beside
local collapses, I trust
no accusation of breach,
it was always given pause

a lank contrail (inceptive)
contains a dropgate, the
least of it tailing
away from its rigid

pitching the breach of
main creation done,
unoceanically
slender in fault

15

Meagre sums clog their
broad calibre, meek
billows curl in the breach

numerous strong streams but
only swaying in rift

the lie of nature behaves (re-
poses) in breaks in the zest

such runs exist where
they can be foreshortened,
corrugated, the shape's complicity
filters (flutes) in verticals

what remains ill-parted
is the impediment's
unfallen open sky

16

Newly skimped as a tunnelled
body breaches its roof,
following (allowing) the gully

unspacious rift, but
how a meagre *zooms*
from unceasing least

more than choice given
an ill chooser, the
scouring chances of creation

bids the hearth go
prowl, the whole body
very soon turns, even
towards the knot
a narrow crevice is

17

Where it rears another, gives
off slender breach, exempt
gift isn't an outcast
of any return reach

razor-thin intimate election,
gaunt from never chiefly apart

don't give me cavity
rocks, but equal
summit periphery, a
pinned ladder
across the green heights

will risk a fault
seeing its own cliff,
faceable peaks
onshore, marooned but for
a community of scission:
now, offered a pre-
subversible, it kept
observant vault

18

Holding on from one slender
scum (single rift), slanted
but unpatched, provenly
beached, meta-nesting

deposit chinks, where
there is no stretch except
proto-crannying, entrenches
the rich offerable partials,
an entire stricken while

left for thin ground, what
the rift was not, but slow
pickings riven in un-
delayed slants, un-
targeted gift aligned normal

19

Doesn't recede with least
bestowing, must be
vowable, a concentrate
of rift, as the prayer-
ful swarms into it

reversion an amplifiability
in the fissure, simply
these rock prows
at their emergent
quota of flotation,
a cluster of com-
binent unriddances
well slighted at pitch,
a niche of retention

a stone dropped in the split
wouldn't identify
but does companion
what lies
cracked by rift

meagre pastures
hem the draw
until sloped enough
from surface drain, so
loads rind, the
patience of gulf
slanting in givens

20

Breached unleaked, a
relation of receptors or
no recapture: striations
of rapid source

slant sting of premature
healing, or how a wheeling
creation hones its groove

the gulf's unending scope
will be abyss-canted,
not dropping off
scrape once granted
a rifted-between

the breach harshly dug out,
scarcely anything's refuge
but unbarely, now
crested below finer shavings:
what divided was
shaft (all frontage)
of impact gift

21

Least *adds*, so let rift
bargain (curtain) with defeat,
does revet (touch) the difference

the centre is poked by
shielding a skinny stick

past rift lies an avenue
into the long crouch,
along it for all treeless
steepnesses above

endure an outskied
breach, plead joy
at a full connection
meagre in leap, but
pushes to the chief stalk
of what feeds the gap,
slanting across
tenderer ground than
given (rifts) enough

A VERTICAL PIERCES, SWATHE IT IN STEM

2016

For Emma Mason

Expressed as a vertical; not *upright*
precisely; *vertical*; intersection
without disseverance

Geoffrey Hill

Earth grown old, yet still so green…

Inner swathing of her fold

Christina Rossetti

La terre
Rêvait donc aussi
De la verticale

Qu'elle fonde les arbres

Guillevic

seen ~~pierced~~ furthest horizon
open to shoreness by sheerness

Mark Dickinson

Note

Is there a way poetry can re-approach the vertical, not so much as a logical or metaphysical absolute, but in a less equivocal, *ie* post-enigmatic, spirit? The question itself sticks at the enigmatic but its lyric provocation projects a stem probing until the latter is itself pierced by an encounter already more than pre-mysterious.

If materiality affords any horizons at all, they effect a swathing both continuous and contrary, a swathing which thrives amid a tall flicker of stems waving and oscillating diagonally. The gift of such givens offers a multi-planar intimacy, a relational distance to be further internalised, a finite constant (no longer the sums of itself) on behalf of.

Sources

Michael C. Kalton, 'Green Spirituality: Horizontal Transcendence', in Melvin E. Miller and P. Young-Eisendrath, eds., *Paths of Integrity, Wisdom and Transcendence: Spiritual Development in the Mature Self* (2000).

Michael Marder, 'The Life of Plants and the Limits of Empathy', *Dialogue,* 51. 2 (2012), 259-273.

Emma Mason, 'All green things': Christina Rossetti's Franciscan Ecology (2015)

John Milbank, 'The Eight Diagonals' in his *The Legend of Death: Two Poetic Sequences* (2008).

Various readings of the 'vertical' from essays in *Studies in Christian Ethics,* Sage, 1988-

If a vertical prayer once
pierce, swathe its uncoat-
ables across stem

swathes in the wild
are a very steep giver

pierces into allowing
bulb, the slim involute,
inhabits a stem over
any ratio of injection

stem towards pulling
from sparsity of root,
detector amid bundle

with self-scanting pierced
by an unconditional, the
trajectory shoot
lances reception

where a vertical pierces
this was stem healing
off tatters of ceiling

a vertical path tenses
no other additionals, the stem
supplement in every
other way shaftless

tipped for a piercing,
gleans verticals from
its own unsteering stem

pronaturals of the vertical,
gift will trans-accord

stem, along each
singular linear rebuff

what pierces to land
not simply the earth
in vertical section
but its horizon's intake

stout to vertical,
lifts off slimmer laterals

a nest of fine earth,
prone stemming interveined,
vertical axis swings up baseline

in angulars gleaning
verticals, a singularity of
upright absorption, piercing
is coiled thread or swathe,
rootal upward stance

transfixes the instant's
byplay, counter-slippage to
horizontal placing is shift
without revision, least rippage

flutings along
a vertical seam
owe to shelter
their vertical niche

vertically aligned
planar ditches, their face
an aperture from
gaunt stems at anchor

scarce completion still
undulates the award of
unsurrenderable slant
but slenderly easable,
how vertical fastening
grants internal sleeve

a tuning stem towards,
after which roots testify
their unadjustably
nurtured turn

vertical not homo-
geneous, intimal contra-
shiver, upper line ally
at sharp shelter of horizon

to be singular-direct,
there is no vertical serpentine
for diagonals to collate

spare horizontals glancing
(not swirling) *onto* verticals
of the offer, the stem
placemat is solar

versal (outpouring)
off lateral stance:
setting a vertical
affords it horizontally
but not its initial
arrival on stem

single-welling offerings,
ascriptive simplicity,

attachment of leaves
at a collarless vertical

singular fathoming off
creation where sheer
horizontals would protrude
multiples of flattening

dynamic fields cultivate
predictive stems, the
earliest future

vertical probe, received
into the singular but as
switch once tripped, re-
opens at narrow stem

lowest co-polar scatter
meets vertical incidence
whose vector is a hori-
zontal bar tilting its
stop-point, fully
pierced open plane

pre-occur at a singular
accord, givens
onto givenness

flame of the ferm-
entation will have
bleaked out,
suddenly an earth-hit,
unfreezes afresh
in stem

there was no vertical goad
but simplified damage-sharing
pacifying the uptake

between two horizontal
stillnesses, their verticals
register in thirds

scant separates on common
low stem avoiding set
swerve, an anterior vertical
greets singular verve

no vertical stretching,
the pull sculls along
horizontal pool, sust-
enance off the
slightest stem-lag

porous at an unpicked
tip, singular renewal
modally ripe

extreme physical information
a flash of realigned occurrence,
the matrix blinks vertical

a stem without root to stern, tapers
at vertical wash, no
further plurals can beset
singulars in this
piercing direct

crosses over lacking mesh,
horizontals won't gear
onto a vertical: adoption

among the givens less
any adaptation

don't fade out the earth
as paradisal mislocalisation

stems switch to reception
which doesn't stack, no
such bare contexts of lack

stem without interminables,
whatever was conducted to a
vertical piercing only stays
finite in swathes

seams of ascension foster
the fuller stem scansion,
stresses a tallness
unfloated, coated

horizontal incisions (con-
cessions) extenuated by
vertical spines

vertical bounds (the open)
did flare at a crack in tip,
fully lipped once swathing
the penetration

stems only go vertical
from not co-spiring
to shed the horizontal

no original sky-stem
until pierced, then came
horizon's composition
in greens

vertical within tissue isn't
spike emergence, each stem
spindles all the way to
root, piercing offers
plant its slender foot

emergence along stem
beyond the velocity of
taper: finite flow of
reality in indiscrete
flaw, floods a super-
added touch of a
vertical poor

singular linen of leaf, a
least-paired common in-
ducement, the linking
vertical, its ranking
shared horizontal

stem-as-leaf pilots
with vertical exaggeration:
once pierced will recognise
a stolon has landed

emergent spine becomes
vertically acquitted, no
longer assailed by
laterals in judgment

convergent vertical flux
at an influx of
rising soil density

fields braid the quiet
granules with a lull

of horizon, there stems
outsource horizontal
compacts, dense things
are nomadic only at
vertical thrift

unforeseen vertical impact,
a smaller fork inserted
(seated) in a larger, the
prayer notch

only weakness is autonomous,
moves through each particle
exchange, so precipitating
sleekness of shoot along
unfinishable (pierced) stem

until stem at its falling
fixed line, so to vast
poor of the vertical

a parcelled dura, small
nodes chronically wide,
no sub-vertical canal
as near: planar fore-face
raises a pierce-stem ground

probe, push, eventually over-
shoot its growth speed
limit: already a hush of
verticals at their cosmic
silent scenics: humility
of a minute repletion
on behalf of

less than us to which
we promise the less of us:
enter a non-dominance
of vertical elation

it cannot be less than us,
we are found with it, as
a less *for* it, so as to pass
into and through it

until the poverty of its
horizons is unconditional,
vertical community
offered to fragile
commonality

vertical transcendence the
bolder lesser, a vertigo
that sustains the en-
compassing, held
to a rippling stem

our occasional particle
in passing through, not
just the temporals of it
but praying the entered
granules between

the stem with its faltering
taper, conductor and
sheath of the vertical

this tip-swathe counter-
predicts its own in-
determinacy anthem

meanest crust of stem
appointing its horizon-
surface vertically prone

are short spurs off stub
accomplishing (divagating
with) vertical ribs

without crest watches over
the frail surface grist of us,
pierces to slender dilations

a human interlude on this
planet (eventual cosmic
disappearance along old expansion
spirals) will have been vertical

calculus by naturals implicates
horizon, self-ascriptive casting
onto explanatory chance, that
parched infinite zero regain-
number as communicants
among ungiveables

dual-swathe fanbeam,
array of diagonal arrival

in relation to a slight
stunning of earth's
intermittency

green at its diagonal
ascendants, sensing a
vertical co-insistence:
own accurrent tensing,
imbricate fan, axial uplift,
prone at-stem patience

so purified by and from,
so swathes the income
of a pierced (charged)
despair

now a disrepair of
interstellar auto-
silences, a frayed
reception: gift's ex-
ception by no
naked recapture

immodest greeting is the
humility of having become,
its deeper poverty,
post-frugal

drawn off the vertical
but never post-perm-
eable in stem

pierce the very chosen weak
point, span columns to
horizon though without
any kit capping an al-
ready foreshortened taper

until the swathe is oval,
domal, pierced vertical,
draws coverable commons
off a no longer
flatly global

swathing per forest of
delayed intimidation,
planet-thorough
penetrates intimation

only this vertical
fully exposes us
to our contingent
swathing, both
piercing us, and it

diagonal roots gave
straight stem along
borderless spans, a
human scale of per-
turbation, anticipation:
unfused, unrefused, pro
co-surgent in prayer

IN ARBOUR TO ABBREVIATION

2016

For John Milbank

Á la mémoire de l'auteur de *Du Domaine*;
in memory of the author of *80 Flowers*

For Hamann...in the tradition that human beings participate in the creative activity of the divine *Logos*, there is...a paradoxically given 'extra' which constitutes humanity. Humanity...writes always in the 'abbreviation' of *hieroglyphs* as if weaving 'on the underside of the carpet'... Creation, therefore, through man and the power of God, writes an abbreviated, hieroglyphic version of the divine pictograph. By writing this hieroglyph humanity is constituted *as* human.

John Milbank, *The Word Made Strange*

abbreviative not
abstemious   clump-tender
where not stunted,
such candid trench

inference is visible
abridgement in
all branches, abbreviant
hazard the whole derivation,
deviates from the obliterate

self-organising
towards
abbreviation,
shortly no
retaliation

abbreviations less
of an element
than every component

brief tree, co-
glistens at the
short-scope
hieroglyphics

a brevity excitement
dressing the contraction,
abbreviant towards
trans-finite

an arbour's chasing
abbreviates markers
(long in tree)
in found swirl.
Its body's adjacent
cope, a sudden copia
to lessen these knots
against contraction

at full length but
fallen into ellipse,
no natural strategy for trees
apart from this
portion elation

in the straits of
wrong frond   a lean
truncation rights
the arbour flow

select to a span
brief stretchers, no such
swarm of narrows
is spareable

brevity combining
repose, recourses
concise specifics,
only diagrammatic
at eventual
improvisatory calm

the shooting mass
abbreviates to an
accord of provision

the trellis of a tree
at the seating
of its knee

tree-walking forest
transducer   to a
depth of backtree,
minute combination
steps up range

cardinality of tree
an exit no longer
in use, abbreviates
supposed evictions

so waving the trellis-
work none too soon,
oscillates its prone
foreshortening

this is abridgement's
counter-span, not
universal cladding's
opponent

greeting (less
meeting) the sprig bounce,
abbreviates a bunch,
abets a leap

exfiltration as
shorter form, once
redispensed the pencilling
will have been ample:
what is left out
makes for a
minority return

where recession is
the hieroglyphic,
withstand the clamour:
abbreviation is fully
traceable fraction
of horizon: if given
it always overtook us,
now freshly open
to the deceleration

clusters (blisters)
on the spur of a
sudden lesser growth's
acuteness

detected into arbour
downface undivided at
an allayed incompletable

gardens at a rare
stillage, the returns
are spare loops
of brevity

axis-light foliage,
fragile stood sheen
hooped to leaf nodes

clear leaves within
booth, acquits a shallow
hoard of shelter

quiet limes in
reserve, abbreviation is
also acceleration: of
relatives, purgatives,
unconditionals

scant is deviant
plenty, recoils west
vestment across
eastings of leaf,
arbour and
devout shanty

the arbour's pursuant
membrane, all shorting
at a tree's circuit
contrivance

these foliage flukes
run to abbreviant barb,
intense leafage
less woods

thrifty with overleaf
the awning is temperate
sanctum, ranked as
less than its source

abbreviatory not reticent,
prickly with concession,
lets such neo-concisions
be far inflected,
need not now be
so sparely detected

intricacy of lack
forever niche-hunting:
keen relation abbreviates
tissue, troubles it
with ligature, some co-
snagged donatory issue

branches are reeds,
alterant veins hollow
to roof, thicken then
on a steer of leaves

too slight a nearage
to be cruised, ultimate

distance will abbrev-
iate itself

bluish leaves adduced
from green city, lately
a sky to arbourside

props of wood lodge,
poling gutted storm,
stringy omissions,
turbulent recession

where leaves abbreviate
there incurve is neither
husk nor splint

in unwithdrawn mid-
hollow, the winter's first
fragment already
planted out

some plummet in leaf-
provision was attested to arbour,
its shortest mutuality

spent leaves inflate
lattice, carry its reduction
which now blows con-
figured towards all

sprinter to green
accomplice, apprentice
abbreviation

no further purging
of the slights of bud,
the arbour is already
a tree-flower's
silted inheritance

earth's abundance
put to its raw dens,
abbreviated enough
for navigating
tides of sift

what can only wilt per
segment is already
a contrary abbreviation,
doesn't abstain from
any hunch of settlement:
the arbour offers
shrinkable immunity,
has enough briefing
afloat in armature

old home-sites aspire
inquiring thicket, not
stung but a fresh node
on abbreviation

this forest test conducts
marks of arbour trans-
mitting a hieroglyphic
prescindent to centre,
each symbolic periphery
makes a nil redundance

template punctual dots
rap (drape) the templum

what greens question of a
cosmos can't be huge:
braid the course of a zone,
shorten its rods to
sourcing off crown

paradise went dim to
overt sheathe,
astute abbreviation
(prayer's referent)
renewing all

free walls span dense
rooms, each iteration
a leap to sanction,
prevenient accession

strips urban miracle
from grace of forest,
a static arbour gone

into all weathers, abbrev-
iant prayerful projection

nursed woods at their
minority threshold,
omissions of growth
(frontiers of advance)
straddle the
zonal prayer

tree-cladding at its
repentance of vest
dresses a short-code space,
long-zone prayer

an evergreen splinter
will connect
unreaped arena:
arbour has no other
harvest
than arising (un-
ripped) from this

how strong is a green coat
to the risk of prayer?

the mask is not adamant
in arbour, its trellis
the shortest way

constantly at a distance,
no longer than the way
offered
its abbreviation

EMERGENT HABITS: NEAREST DRESS FAR OVER TREES

2016

Skin of Open Fields, the.
Maggie O'Sullivan

For He hath clothed me with the garments of salvation
Isaiah 61

NOTE

Why does emergence seek an ontological garb? It comes to cherish that radical turn-about which is where emergence has arrived in terms of horizon but isn't yet what it has come to be: the intimacy of a further participatory outcome of gift no longer or not only the progress that has been travelled, resisted or diverted, but what emergence is dressed in, a leading counter-current of receptiveness. Taking ontological aim at deepest (uneven) relief, this heuristic unbrokenness of canopy becomes a universal sequence.

The phrase 'emergent habits' is derived from *How Forests Think* by Eduardo Kohn (2013).

Emergent habits
from counter-habitual,
dressed for unfamiliars
one more attiring

the cocoon of outspread
quickens a loosened
unloser, throw
a scarf's

how a scurf of trees
extenuates, tempers
the emergence

clothes us in frail fabrics
unscrambling horizon
with seeing scars,
a thatch of spars
below their watch
of semi-stars

lagging ahead of the mut-
ilated, fostered to its
crooks, gives replenishment
shawl by shawl

no tree simulacra
inciting the swerve from field,
veteran neck turns in-
ordinately round scarf:
bypassing the cycle gives

emergent nub, one offer
on from saturate hub

not always succinct in adhesion, a capacity poor-store bare enough for the jolt of emergence   dresses then what had lost its way from floor: whichever root-bound knows no more branch-zero   re-bestirs a post-avoidance, the layer itself was already speculative

too slight along to have
rested at a blunt touch,
a sheering of counter-shoot
but stunted (sprinted)
by invasive variation
at the consentive spark

lapsed overheads dilate
a throw's declination, bring
uprights their preferences
in stubbing   imparted
back to shelter, such thin
permissions stray
to the commutatory

the least glut is some
misfeed foraged towards:
a tree before its scarf not
so much draped as dropped
on a designatory   benign
baffle as inceptional sock
coats the annexation

scarce crumbs of nature
at its horde's seasonal
office of not now
crowding out
the canopy of prayer

not treelessly put to the edge of
copse, erring from stand to
grove, from canopy to ambient
blowing scarf   where
shocks of emergence
leave a cluster

a leaf one of its selves towards a wave of scarf, not yet a leash of fabric   no
secular clump gathers this emergent profile   the oak's sediment ripped
from hierarchy, wrap *that* in the scarf's flare   wading an emergence dries
towards waddage, slowly to irrigations of prayer

pray across the unshadowed,
what a texture of tree-dress
(penetration's duress) won't
have had to thin out to

amplified remotely, in-
timately comparisoned shoot
over root   such caparisons
thread the emergence,
embed symmetrical
resurgents

no canopy at its projection's
straits without re-darting
(pre-dating) a slend-
erly set emergence

leaf in tandem to
future coating, outseed
joins in retro-habit

perspectival annunciation is from time's new access towards the recess advancing the fabric   what surges as alternative limb is the trees' unmown emergence, no conveyance without canopy, no nearer than waiting under eaves

thimble origins get nested
within indices of extension,
a tiny dome goes on being
pinned down but shares
the furthest reach

inter-ascendant foliage
in mutual uncertain
curtain, those contaminants
press to shelter, brush
more than they can harbour
on horizon but stay for
one more net of the garment

verticals where they didn't
greet me further, but
instant density of the en-
trance granted shelter

by such scarce means emer-
gence covers a ground but
won't revert to it, clothes
one finer twist of remove

green elision of a universal
turn, what is abbreviated onto
screen is elongated by an
uncompact refracted rapture

recesses which counter
the occlusion, allow
containment its billow

what emerged is re-
offering the crabbily hatched

not as improvement but at
a reproofing, micro-
roofs a tangent
over fragment

unrequitable gift
stained through and through,
filtered at the soak
of its habit

unenclosed or gapped
in sediment, this matches
a green scarf to
silts of horizon

pushes time from
impeded same duration,
dress deserves phase,
a backing seam
to tuck the proviso

from every
tie-back due bar one:
that each radial
stretch of frame
co-press (address) the reach

no further encampment
but a future encapsulates,
a bubble of prescience
arising from the previous
meniscus-field

spread to its newest
non-nakedness in
ordinary unfolding

fling piercings together
but dress the contusion:
damage and exposure
acclimatise a riper scarf
than themselves

emergency is the having become
prayerful, bowers
its abrasive screening
of the weakest acute

continual emergence of
lineage, seep of forest,
poverties strong with life
which trees amplify
and redress, learn the garb
out of this much

not zigzagging litter
off a tree apportioning
the cull of feature
but rooted in a call legacy:
tangent replacement still not
absorbance's effacement

sighs of emergent spares
unmuffled (prayers) by foliage,
shiver a post-saturate
symbolic, shielding direct
arrived as it out-
dressed the clearing

irreducible unseverable,
horizons disparate in hold
briefly centred at the
return-margin's cover

nested emergent threshold
needs be tested, a modality
of symbolic interference

emergency rough-out
gives a further turn
through any inhaled habit,
selectivity re-tempers
its own projection (pro-
jettison) of texture

realm fitfully decoupled
but repercussant   as in
urgent ephemeral prayer
sustained in recess,
orbital skein of wander-
ing long the winding

a shared upframe over
the world's enter forest,
began to co-flank
its shadings

particles misapplied
give to history its
canopies of revocation,
narrative detracts under
a welter of para-event

a host of trans-thoughts lend a species to prayer, no generals except shy
incommensurate relata   supervenient, hyper-primitive   all too privative
unless coating the excess   dresses it in a poverty of unconditional access,
escorting prayer along its meta-palpables

seed-scale according to
a tarnish of leaf-scarf:
dual-phase emergence,
refine the removals and
relayer the growth

a caritas among the
not-yet transformed,
interacts a whole al-
ready with its missing
parts, now emergence
inhabits lesser-towards

press no subfunction
but adjacent verticality,
prayer's addressable
lattice slant-gained:
this leaf-coating is not
imitative register

how forests think forward
their banking on shelter,
any lumpen whole is the
greeter of the located
scum of its parts:
something else is redress
for a nothing but

branches already in being
hang over our opening, a
paucity sensing controvertibles
between closures of becoming:

hard encounter will promote
corrugated symbol

the dependency gives its
minute impact declaration,
set to a roof unachieved-re-
coverable: by which our
self-organisings are other-
prayered, screened
post-fractive

let emergence be a wholescale
revision of the earth's crust,
tuft of air sought in
tail of leaf, winged against
unlatticed retorts of roof

is not a plate of
existence but a surface
in service of all other
covers, such layering
a horizon hovers for

subunits assign super-
strates of heuristic shelter,
how an angle bonds, supports,
by forking across the whole
nil-reprisal tangle

emergentist velocity
at which its naturals

reframe taciturnity,
forward recess arises
from the sullen bunker

in woods always that other rooming for what would twist the knot were
emergence sheer spiral   but not abstaining from a less inventive, now
each veil of the slide to species overshoots its texture but is carded looser
(combinable) at the inter-bestowal

though still assailed by
substrates short-circuiting,
the catalyst canopy
can't simply prevail:
its habit only a slight
friction of the emerged
no longer
stark meditational

a site-diffidence of out-
zones, each bias serves
a boundary-skin from
previous inversions

flawed shells gleam
at recurved orbitals,
the new incompleteness
circulates as prayer

mutates the range of
what is *in* range, no
adjacent stretcher element

the same shored awning
offered novel combinatorial
attentions: from its ancient
leaf family to a cascade of
reorgans, none parades
an ex-vestiture

a thin virtual realm not
scaling material outcomes:
entire scale makes for
deckle of leaf, radical
dapple of symbloid
welcome

at the summit of these emergents is a chapel of never having travelled the distance (dia-stance) but been overtaken by it   given once only, poverty of outcome is the sole remainder compound of success, offers a nothing further adjusting its here, working the salience of being struck to an unconditional

clamour of self-guidance
in prayer no longer sent
its auto-silence: to be
racked with gift whose
apex emergents improvise
a cry within their until

a vein of shallow super-
scape out of which we
have aimed the subsoil,
a tree's multizone domain
of protraction, recessed

along rootal repairs
of diagonal spoil

what was given to the
self-organ to selve
its horizons, incoming
autonomy from a diremption
it had not divined

will put in rotary section
what could follow such a before:
emergence is what is there to
be dressed in, no sieve
apart from its lattice grant
seeking a para-habit

what has canopy
negotiates cosmology,
emergent etherials pose
their material events

would cross-infuse
assistances of incon-
sistency, a rewilding
homogeneity of register:
deep liturgy of erring
enough for a steering

cherishable flux is offered
the flotation it can only
tack to variables on behalf,
fleeting-with a time-for

to be steeply enmeshed is not to surpass ordinaries of the sacral   gift
places such steeps in ritual curiosity   forgoes them in greeter radiance,
steps up acutest prayer

a foliage model over-
vaulting the sealing,
this came to be
no naked healing

reciting the geostory
in sure frank surplus,
out to a further coping
of the go-inception

funds a mental earth
trembling before life,
emergence is layer
appalling layer

shares agency with other
losses, with future non-
autonomies of hampered
combination, fully repairs
(bears) its habit

untamed but open de-
votedly, a universe's
rinse of selection, its tiny
cell by cell eclection,

multiplies a world
primal of a few
ample donor objects

the fragile envelope quakes
into staying with prayer's
deliberate inhabitant

because a phusomorph
embraces non-identical agency,
its own self-shelter appoints
it showing such protection,
re-prays the autonomy

tree structures that print, ab-
solve, human verticals on the
world, each substantiation
interpreted by its previous
future, become already
having been to be

deep shelter home
to the barenesses of prayer,
leaf-sifted (a para-lift) from
barrenness: porous
habits unadjourned,
sufficiently micro-exposed

how does a host of nature
take the vertical cut
as the seams of its
very habit?

premised on life, the con-
tingency provider
divides at prayer:
this addressable has no
biotic undress

ENCLOSURES

1983

To isolate the kernel of
Our imbalance and at the same time back up carefully;
Its tulip head whole, an imagined good.

Ashbery

Losgelassenes kreist, und sind wir auch selten die Mitte
einem der Kreise: sie ziehen um uns die heile Figur.

Rilke

the needful things are a sacral
convergence, the grove on
a hill we know too much of

Prynne

1

To enter amenably with a set of prospective inclusions, expect the surround of shelter to be post-gated, across a line of upright rails, over a window of horizontal rails. Across the wires and over the pipes and in at receding conversion.

What is entry into enclosure if not to be coiled in its paling, ravel up the skirting of what departs enclosure wind-chequered and heath-exposed? I only enter in with out. Companionable since I can't negotiate the enclosure at all except lined in its skin, the studded circuit of the outside. I may prick but obtain only needle and gap without reconcerting images. I foresaw duality but not the thin asymmetry of accompanying outline.

Nothing on the inner side is imaginable immediately post entrance, to enter is to be unreminded of any discrete alignment by which an inside nests in the outside. Only an image for the fact of enclosure which in the act of entering becomes a surface curled and unextendible, a delivery of rolls without rules for lay. Delineation is furled but expanse refuses to contract and also accompanies. I'm kept alert by the unilateral images of entry, always familiar, uncertain as to which way the outside is no different, suddenly inopportune as unbroken.

It expected to be focused out, the plain of out bridged and ditched in a naïve frieze but is no smaller, hardly trifled with. Entry is simple repetition of everything that expected to be sacrificed. I acted as though abandoning open flyless Mogshade for the close shade of Oakley, to file through whatever fault in itself the open allows, but the open simply followed whatever was entered, accepts selvage which the pines don't reinforce, not binding banks, not contracting water lesions.

No effort, the most easeful post-creation I've ever walked into, a post-creation of walking into. I may be slightly cushioned, the pegs of enclosure underscoring the limit of vision but no nearer. Though to be aware of diminished flaccidity, the gate (not to be looked back at, not knowing how an inner side appears) must have disappeared behind a bend in the ride. The possibility of turning within an enclosure may be the first affirmation of enclosure even if not identifying any direction, though possibly the portable weight of the outside may have veered a little.

It was a texture got me slightly past a corner where what isn't used to being seen (were I to have looked for the inner rail) doesn't have to be seen and wasn't after all searched from. Affirmation realises the economy of enclosure. As if the outside were almost itself situated were it not for being without situation at a point where the inside is within, two asymmetries looked for beside each other, hoped for by naming their possessions. Only within enclosure is what contains enclosure imaginable, how easily the outer fencing slipped in alongside. But entry discloses I only imagined myself looking at what I took to be contained, taken in by the placation of being enclosed. The inside isn't itself disclosed, only re-enclosure of the tags and reminders of the whole appearance.

If what I came in from is already contained by what I'm come into, I'm only trying to concert images for re-entrance, to cope with a convention of the within restationing its own images of the without. I'm not trying to surf at banks and palings from within a delectable crosslight of equivalent pine-needles, to cheat them by making substantial a translucence based on the other side of whatever their locations may oppose against me. Rather, I'm being further detained within a sphere around which outlines were induced which was always ready to reduce its competence in order to decipher a shape for entering by, though with the hidden promise of eventual re-entry in company with its own appearance. The enclosure though seems to offer dependence by being rigidly available, perhaps as more willing to align the two asymmetries. In the triangle of re-entry it offers itself as a third grade to horizon, a frame against which a within within may be no more difficult than a without without, the stirring still out there somewhere in a wiry dependence of neighbourhood. But the dependence requires caution and is rightly enclosable.

To advance amenably: padding along a neighbourly line which services via swaying points that inject the line what is enclosed by and what encloses. Advance is linear, I take it I can choose to think of being here, spectate around inside having brought in with me a culpable within bearing landcast faults of the professing without, distinguishable rucks which in near identical terms are permitted their old autonomy as opaque frames.

The repeated within of a secondary containment is in the accompanying light of the repeated without, a refrain of the conflating impasse of enclosure as it solders compass. Repetition incomes the linear, highlighting the paths, sidelighting the runs and gulleys of lodgepoles, wide-swathed as fronts and sides uncomplicate analects of direction. I may speak again without such danger, net the inside without exclusive reference to gates and embankments, merge (or simply lift out) theme and allusion. In this straight march I never thought to take I treat the inner rail as identical with the outer rail, or rather as though the outer style repeats itself in a blank space imaged as the deferred within regained by the outer lesions it always contained.

Advance invites the ahead which is outside, but enclosure softens the aspiration to deferred outlet. It appears to be drifting laterally through mudbanks, swaying as if linear sightlines really underlay it, mimicking which convention cites which, as if containment were arbitrary, wings and flaps of encasement huge and pungent tucking up tiny directional sinews, the garish cockfeathers of enclosure overhanging sober external priority by corpulently massing against it. Two asymmetries of space in a meeting of endless conventions, which as conventions are symmetries, as endless endless.

The thematic of a name pointbound as the point of you, plenitude of a name bearing nothing but broken into place, a blockage convention is to have something by which not to go further. To allow you is opening an enclosure into you. The incision no more reference post entrance.

2

Reality, comfort, hoped for in discrete alignment, reflexive nesting, well up against the transfixer. You who opened the flow insist it's solidifiable now, here against the existent side of your name, the chooser's stream, where caravan features blockade the ground, attract into viscous grades. The real parks in moats, its lesions trickling at comfort on the plain of the outside where you drove a presence that stunned its hemless location. Now nothing passes under or over, conventions of the outdoors reroute around you scouring ditches that don't describe you. But prevent the loss of inscription.

I thought nothing evaded it, nothing overlay the planisphere. Where your face makes cipherless rings not being sutures it wouldn't heed them other than as a painless flotation of ringstops and endstops. I believed the outside had no way of not going further. But the plain slips at indecipherable modes of re-entry. As you return from your token of emergence you won't abandon what made it out, description so visible that far outside. It wells round you now, enclosure a contravention of not being into, ballasting evasion into the dividing instant simultaneous you.

Desire slewed by space but desires the body's fractionality, the emplacement twined among identical limb displays, almost too solipsistic a symmetry of body by body inviting to the brief centre, a make-ready of nesting. Not sparing a kind of less-local, the offbreathing of speech which in casting mist upwards/downwards paths it, handy inside/outside, voicing an embraceable way back to displacement, linear limbs by which we solidify space, reply outlying dividing skirts, the nether side more truly blank for inhabitation.

Where once I didn't ask you splayed over a book which you'd isolated from circulation, into the early morning the body wriggling through the screen of reading you introjected, trying to be frame-distended and steady but at once needing to diffuse bodily inventiveness capacitating its own projections, wagging at territory.

What you delected was non-proliferation of space, unfeline, a flicker of registration, lection of becoming behind the formality of a day's flesh clearable as apple-muff, the modesty of phase-relation. Cheeks, ears, hairline, concentric rings you make off with—outing circuits but not spinners only—a slight tapering of nose and hillocks of eyes, exist suddenly in no relation, are inapposite descriptions, not the geometry of any groundface but what you abandon at every moment, temporal not as procedure but as endstop, the self from which. The breadth of face and slope of poll are retained but invitations of lesser angles by which the face was inhabited recall the brief centre and are consumed by recall.

Summoning your weathering presence in a drifting climate contours of effort dilate. Whose mind bathes on an allowable surface then? But were I to brush you at such a moment you would record only beakiness, palings. The assignments of outline go drily onwards, finitive wires trailing the roomy ground they endclip, pre-emptors of a mushy immerging of self into copious other just as warily demarcated. And these don't loosen unless marginally let be. The equipment of enclosure was all too faithful to what you skirted, its team-strings interlaced with replete precision whatever tackle you threw away, drily inclusive of whichever repeating surface you broke up in the outside.

You recorded being empaled groundhogging opaque, felt an invasion accompany and fit discretely, collecting into itself what it didn't describe.

You'd rather have been streamed over, not been avoided courtesy of nominalising enclosure which is beaky in not confusing you with itself. You'd rather have mocked inapposite images and raced into the surplus. No way of showing I tried to allow that too without your having let the palings trail right up to you, housing you as another place but to be taken in by you as delivering yet again its circling-off. Those palings that recognized you from within whatever they contained recognized you only from within it, the enclosable blankness. But seeming to know you before you passed through into what then represented them was to you self-reflexive, a self you might mark yourself at but not the self from which, self of secret access to the chequered outside (it's the outside which shelters) disbounding among signed parts and settlements of yourself, interstices secretly not self to self but if as fluently negated by another marked as violation, empalement.

Certainly it was the succulence of interstices I took, but not as a map on which to graph cooled bones shorn of projection, induce presence from absence and then discard the absence, but rather to meet you along the way such a mutuality might be broken down, stream over common asides since you are ahead of what you accompany, not offset by but among what you are not, outlines remembered only by way of discarding a convention of not knowing, where you discard the light of being known, two facts of passage which as passable conventions drift without increase, as knowable knowable.

You walked ahead as the sequence towards the site is, having been beside what was coming beside me as if at the common root but that's unimaginable, hardly conceivable on a path being serial. Along the path in a preverbal infilling of space, a taleless trail, your stun of location walked along location. What is simultaneous is the equal originality of sequence.

You were already in the wood when I came down the hill, half-hidden but not enclosed by it, it bore only the landscape mark of passing between, coastal beside the path's increscence. This is mid-enclosure, no more reference to gates post entrance, irrecoverable where features deny their element in a pure shift of the same. It wasn't we were at different points simply uncovering the same intervals. After, before, in line, are common roots on the path only if in extension, and extensions become conventions of no meeting, only as conventions simultaneous which on a path is unrepresentable, but healing the temptation not to know or the fear of being known. Removing the apposition of either.

The path is extension in one, unpairable, always putting itself into the way of becoming itself which is a highly restrictive use of centre without recourse to periphery or reflection, the simultaneous not surpassed but displaced into its own intention, curvature unreturning.

At mid-enclosure only unrepeatable passage is containable. On line with you isn't having to differentiate between you and not knowing you, where you're the same reflex whether stripped as solid or projection. The literal as re-vented, regained by conventions not themselves represented. Re-externalisation has to stratify if the figure letting go isn't to drip back down the neck. Reduction towards outline, midprocedure in company of bylines, the wood safe as wood whether at Oakley or here in what you walked between, that real stream of wood not named or internalised, its features latticing steps to guarantee the continuous hold of no meeting tapping out sequential root.

The seriality of the path is a difficult joy, a passing good like an unmirrored greeting without areas of symmetry, meeting by means of repetitions unexchanged.

3

An enclosure into which you never walked, not providing your absence or presence but a usable path loosening at midpoint, not simultaneous with you, no dividing instant, simply turnable into as many rides off fresh gravel.

Middle may lose time, only the sharpness of entry makes it seem overprompt but once in there's no further principle of division, it may prove the smallest kernel or a tedious bloat but no offmid, inmid, outermid.

No exits to or entrances from you here, not enclosure nosing round offlines where you're the original fault, giving all priority to what's unconverted into you then tucking back into itself the strips of extension halted, though only in a derivative manner, by you, not enclosure as ejection: not so much even a place where you don't count, to be idly addressed from, but having its amenable grammar, playful separations and reruns inventing no sources, no longer familiar with the hiveholes in or out, simply the middle of from or towards into which the outline of enclosure billows, skittishly holds nothing against being unbrokenly visible.

I can select one of several lanes without looping where enclosure invents enclosure, not as recycling but as counter-named extension: from Oakley along to Beech Bed. If the middle's in extension it too has some sequence which may make the rings of enclosure unreturning. As such I'd taken a distinct left turn off the main drive through tracks becoming wider, pool-like but with the mildest linearity unrepeating, direction webby through the consequential but unregulated map of trees, though the beeches are compacter in blocks which as blocks drift a little above a slight undertow, honeysuckle and sorrel, or across the inserted current of diminutive oaks.

Douglas firs don't set the edges of the ride, don't suture the outer ruts, but match only as vertical headings requiring a further horizontal in blue air above the beeches which they intersect without shadow or any powdering of texture. Individually they're the vices which socket black moss and blue air together without gradations of block texture, without blockage, living in the offsets of the beeches not as borderers but as runners of the across into the upto, resetting shelves of soil other trees and sky (which for the beeches had been a play of stacking the vertical horizontally) into uprights, not selvages or sentries but overplaying the invisibility of the path's endstop horizontal into a visibly vertical stop at crown: the play of ending in midpoint where the intermediate disguises its continuations, teases the security of middle by imitating the cut-off of gates and ditches of no more reference until what they're not yet up to.

An affirmation of enclosure not just where your absence isn't reduced to presence, but a stop-off of the within and the without where they're both in the midst of continuing, where you could be if you so wished represented. I may speak again without such danger here where conventions aren't disturbed by lack of functionality or on being apprised are conventionally so, exposed at midquarters, remaining that good way of the woods that hasn't yet secreted evidence of exit lines except in crowns and leading shoots which are unmatchable, too many exits, these deep thickets are no different from outer edges but unreferring. Across which I may be followed by you.

I can't have evaded or invaded you, these web-like rides scratch securely across the plantation, are diagonally at the heart of it, neither towards nor beside, not holding back discretions, not pinpointing projections, can recognize you're essentially subversive of yourself attracting imitative migratory space unburdened here in its phase of mid-enclosure, an undertow pulling against the means by which you belong to yourself. Though here a rerun of boundaries only. Not an infinitely extendible site but one still shuttling the economy of enclosure.

You pursued me into here drumming the path, vibrated its rebecomings into comings at, aimed this retreat making sequences thematic, you stalk as impulsion fired by expansive retreat, down you come through the widening spiral erring towards the vacant whiptail of its centre, this ovalling midpoint where it's you who wished to be loved, wanted this love object to be what you're wanted by, desiring the desirer, middling inversion of the lying off of loss now pursued inwards, your absences myself desired by you.

Or rushing in because no longer original, the free slide of priorities at midpoint—do you still fear interiors cover you, shadow you into coming after? At this point equality is unrepresentable, your derived origin coming in from a diffuse distance finding its source in what it pursues. You began as someone I enclosed but pace me now in the uneven place of discovering being desired is unsituatable down the sprawling midcome of enclosure.

You desire me along subtle breakages of its demarcations (exchange of entrances and exits it has no use of), you pile round desire as the pursuing original, your priority heathwide and sourceless before which I retreat into the narrow kernel of the outside, the paltry ditch and bank of re-externalisation. Where I derive you as a drive to appearance, to deride me from you.

I may as well invade you, praise my aggressor, rerun whatever it is you can be here, no less for being invaded who never needed to be here, following attentively, leaning on my words, in drag as the possessor's possessor. All this is the silence of what is sufficient to you, that unforgivable priority where nothing comes of you, where you've no need of report, no location speaking to location only the offhand priority of absence which I too hold landlessly over you.

What enclosure contains is a close field lacking resistance, holding out a paddied sequence of intent. It's here you wanted me, here you bring my images home acknowledging a love that might as well make you real. In your submitting mid-enclosure defers its own continuations as if each phase were statically representable, a centre stalling on the spindle of desire and not, despite all, the surpassable economy of mid-passage.

Loving me isn't an inversion of distance to be objected to, not here where your absence is also absent, bringing you down a spiral of close beakless trees where you are the desirer from which. But such an accumulation of possessions may require exit. If you can only continue you won't hold to centre, won't be a surrounder but a small body, a small body of, blank inhabitation that stunned location into jilting ring and line, diverting you into the cross-ties of place, here all malleable possessions. If you've ever been a representable desirer you'll certainly insist on continuation to exit now, but those blunt features a little bulbous, occasional ball earrings that saucer the face, all these enclosure rejects as too much of you and leaves them to billow across the middle of the hoarding.

Out on Blackensford Hill the tail reach of North Oakley veers, outer palings reach companionship as if some sort of half-revealed loop of which this emergence is the head pulling them round into side-station, but where it's simply necessary to realign emerging from the obliquity of Beech Bed. All the same they look like preparations for exit, side-lines coming into view though not yet drawing into any final valency. North Oakley at junction still binds sidings of inky firs, spray stoops that wave up sufficiently but are all still securely knapped at base by the ongoing ribbon of enclosure.

Fences may speak again and though the wire is sideless the fences take sides though not meaning externalisation, saying it more as shelter which gets out here or is alongside, emergence out of the poultice of enclosure into enclosure as a laning of space where hierarchy though not discarded runs along parallel furrows, the track itself quite easy and open though stricter than a driftway.

Embankments are some distance off and only trailingly visible to one side. How they turn back to guarantee themselves isn't represented here, the trees they enclose aren't shut away but have become wideside as equal ratios of path. I am alongside whatever ingathers at North Oakley and the longsidedness can be read as enclosure. The outer rail is identical with the inner rail in an intercalation of space down seamrails, enclosure not despising to be recognised as the partial furnishing of a heath which cloggily defers its own difference from encirclement in gorbels of self-sowns, the ragged pineforks of Stinking Edge (true to the side of things) or the cossetted turntabling of diminished Bratley Wood now without the certainty of inviting or expelling, a fantail of edges drifting off-centre that turn as thinly out to in as in to out.

I'm out of the derivation of midreport, now by sided posts hale for following wide paths skirting very little where the edges aren't ambitious but ooze in transverse section towards Backley Bottom or lead astretch the stubby entrances and exits of small animals over the crossleaf and bell channels which heed elongation at Bratley Arch.

Enclosure seems soft-jointed, not as yet dispersing but curving between thinly moulded continuations, interested in what might be suspected of passing clean through it (those deadly wires), little concerned to tuck in duration or topologically underscoot outlines back through the ring of semi-conscious trees. It would rather conceal its circuits, its all-round competence, and suggest tactile longitudes, a multiform performing as interruption.

4

The vibration of wire between tall stills, dared through oaks at Bratley Enclosure, isn't a hum of fences (by Bratley banks are thrown open) but the snap of traffic at interval frets along a piercing hairline. Continuation careless of its modes has vaunted clean interruption. Not that the road interferes, it rather increases tolerance of enclosure—nothing is given way as outlet, any apparent boundary lies along what it makes for rather than beside it.

Enclosure in reaching across the business of landscape punches through itself a waypipe which like itself is amenable: as penetration lacking imaginable endstop isn't reserved against enclosure always to have been tracked over by the road-sense of paths. Now on the whistling road, leaning into a cutting, is looking at passengers who feel the ringstop, sense travelling never shifts ground between them as they shoot under the headsigns of enclosure seawards or northwards at a gridspeed of what never has to be reached again or was never any further. But how serious is a road-sense which rejects transformation and not quoting a surface will have nothing going to be understood?

Is the road an exemplum against travelling, the facetious continuum of renewal incredulously peered at between trees, or the means by which the modesty of enclosure takes exercise, a contradictory but intermediate convention enclosure allows within itself, talk of travel, spread of cities, clean rubbing down in pillule motion? Or is containment a palliative as the absolute roadband heads through landscape, in outline conforming to the steering-pin but which allows in its way an accompanying convention of soft-shoulders, the projective goal still virile but increasingly decorous over one-night stands which as they intwine bulge into neighbourhoods? Some confusion over which convention sites which.

A bus passes, sights clear of trees, and a perception (if treeless, unclaimed) allows nose diagonally to coat sides into the almost instant seatedness of back, but fording slight shifts of relocation or some remounting of motion, what's little less than clean trajectory but something less than absolute simultaneity. The eye of enclosure requires trifling hindrances as the locatable where in the eye of the road transmission is fixed by moving through.

Were it never any further, were enclosure always overt, it would still need travelling over, a constant exercise of approach minding steerage and the track-location of signs not themselves boundaries and never available to the ground they surpass. Not that the road really does manage exchanges, it isn't paper-light in drawing past itself but like enclosures is a curiously ribbed and over-literal form. But it makes translatable the affair of surface, in that sense can be thought of as being written down, owns the value of the proper slide though even road-sense must suffer a density of equipment, carriage, stock, limited capacities prearranging return journeys.

Houses gain the roadside with the importance of a newly arrived periphery, some new standard of containment demanding influence. But enclose filaments of traffic offroaded for a time only, never become embankments worthy of converting the outside. A line of houses threatens not with a sequence of the within but with alternate endloops of slack retention, twists in the fabric that will always bear further isolation, circlets in which the road is swollen emptying space, unreflexive, not repetitive even. If the end of the road is representable it's where no house invites another.

For the enclosure eye no field of conjunction, for the road eye no follow-on, were it not the enclosure's recurring stance (often revealed in the course of linear ambitions) is amenable to inviting the surface (so subject to building) back into freedom from endless proliferation. A city in love, under the protection of enclosure, wouldn't expend love as future, isn't thematic about loss. The separations take part in slower exchanges, love was before absence already contained in a way becoming less misapplied, its divisions not endless in brisk differentiation but rounding exhaustible signs, not love the traveller.

In the city no evading you. If I were to match your eyes there wouldn't be shame, only some drop-connection which if it signalled at all (as the first-comer off the crowd) would be shelterless and undeviating, the delight closer than perspective, you'd be sited right through such natural overstepping, the screen-sharing of high density where we close in the effect of the nearest.

I wouldn't find you a second time as here where your lights are opaque. The city doesn't compare what it misses, connections which don't take leave no reminders of clothing, no strands of fabric. Or the images which do drop are set down as a bit more traffic, footboards, treadable relations. It's a way of spooling out the flexibility, a continuous line of nylon ways round—the slimness isn't engaging but knows the circuit's range. I'd prefer the liquid waist were liable to sudden hookings-up where, once rerouted like a bank collapsed over a path, whichever direction it untied would be unexchangeable. I'd go back and make better use of what had passed beside: too many interspaces not supportively empty but vacancies already interpreted, filled already with identical material by the first comer in the opposite direction. Between familiar doors should be the territorial number of unentered houses, the gaps between able to taste the featured doorframe. It's how you enter, placed in the correct density of filled and unfilled.

The rice-thin filament of those who recall my name, the sequence of urban biography indexed to make good the gaps in territory, is scarcely load-bearing. In arbitrary squares I arrest my feet, this is not the run of the street, I want my relatives to be non-selective paving, the street before it begins to greet. Though if the city had a principle of location this would be an inapposite description, the grounded not being its makeup. Spoken without much danger, the groundless not descending gratuitous air to be defended. The city's conventions aren't local props, it doesn't touch them by the feet, or rather, its conventions are enclosed against it.

It doesn't recall self making anything of self through a texture of objects or bars of surface intending whole clusters of its momentum, single posts for a lengthy grammar of traffic that have a way of stabilizing representation—it returns reflexiveness, a full measure of perspective to which objects don't cohere, the state of its own production. City of incessant circulation lacking a non-operational spine submerges its circularity, outlines go under, there's only the static of travelling through, riding the flashing rail where fantasies of limitation are projected against the inner shine, seamless tubes unrenew and uncorrode spoon-drip central heat.

Travelling seated lines the city, underisory tunnels of entercontainment match body seepings where underwear narratives lipread form, occupation for the tented flesh. What casing might that be, what oil of enclosure, the already arrived?

The city is only spoken to in a secondary language, explicatory conventions for revisionary outlines, the home of the second comer. The suburb is superb revision, relativity of elsewhere to which its garden furnitures more decently refer, rice-textured it balloons the city it would rather not enter, swelling the roads into verges, deconstructing the exchange between centre and periphery. Gaspipes sing, leak a little sourly this far out, too far out to come for reparation, on-line you know you're at some loose end but injected with the inexorable centre.

Circuit from which, a skating drum whose outlines you acquire by casting yourself from, into a density of roles with benefit of a little stiffness, position depending on whichever section of the continuum you ejected from—whether to guard over what has no ownership or leave fires in public woods, responsibility as belonging, shamelessness as belonging—whether to extinguish or relight the fireside unattended.

Were you there? I think of you less its sufficiency, but you might have covered the roadway with the handover of a name, towards speculative regulation of the miscellaneous occupied. The reach of the mind is so much built over.

5

Fear uproad. You might be prolonged that way, swept by the beaming freedom of the road into an instantly attachable discovery past old capsules confiding object-delay. Which would then switch you, condense travelling to permanent illumination, you'd be nucleated by the city it always apparently intended.

The road might prove a basic principle if it came with fewer spares. There are no limits to its usefulness, the city depends on being prized open by it even though it immediately gets interned as a wound without edges. Any other discretion limpid in bailed country dissolves into the seamless combs, aerated magic, the injected bubble.

If you came this way, took to the city, you tower over what the rest of us can't keep to, you alone beget readership with something to do in that valley. Insistent transplant of texture into further homes always ripe for the pioneer stage, beansmooth flesh coasting between the empty and the occupiable. The lip where flesh isn't divided between the equal palpability of the clothed and clothing parts is a delicate hairline of fabric across fabric, or the body is a covering which shelters what the city wears.

How texture queues for enlargement, the gantries of precincts and intersection tunnels being the precise touch, the literal scale on peak operation humming gently under a tympanum of flesh on its errands completing the seal. Your ears so well-hemmed are exactly of a size with long-range messages here but this is to sponsor you not as metaphor but as revision.

The shallow tray of flesh even before being marked out as urban vellum had all the translucence of precarious partitioning between practice and groundlessness, now has only enough moisture left to ease the second coming into which the bones dip. Not that such erections claim common office with the struts of the city—they knit flesh the wrong way round—the city deals in amenable post-carnation. It needs texture (a little grit may be added where bones once walked for themselves), a gum of the uncreatable, the already arrived, to objectify its vast accumulation of screenless reflection: celebratory slime to thicken the fabric of provisional tents, super-recoveries to be slackened off from the wind.

We operate the city for one another. Where we're at our most serviceable seeking at least one transposed body in which to site many others reduced to consciousness, that one foreign life might be equally visible, seeable for what sees. In love though I might relinquish the right to surrogate visibility, but the city's all achievement before intent whether companioning or not. Such surrender rolling you up is dazzled by the equal invisibility of strangers. Love wouldn't stick at abandoning its one-sided representative, remain uninformed if necessary on a plot which despite common cultivation in the end has to be cleared by separate gutters. But some angle across it never disavows, which even if not a matter of witnessing discrete harvests has an irreversible imprint perhaps further swarmed by delicacy, the vision however accountable remains usable in other ways. Warmth, especially if it endures, stands on the veridical plain, that certain flatness of intimacy not long for here only.

Unless the views keep moving too. The city's licking it off centre if inhabitable at all, its nucleus an abstraction in which the unsteadiness of the image is already formalized, perceiver of surrogate landscape, distended eyeslick too lubricated for focal nettles. The screen though still descriptive in our hands so that we get off and tour, might become less attentive. We might begin to reabsorb our bodies, the streets something shorter than a retrospective wake.

But the city's eventually good at letting us razzle seeing only very slightly, the rest of the beam overshoots us down the full length of its tube. It provides the incisive projection while we in benign alienation are no more than blurredly in town. It must be presented against us, the unlivable high-focus of embodied consequences, it may be the only economy the city has to offer, all exactness to be accounted for in advance of personal histories, adjustment to life-stages already made. For us a rediscovery of the body's lack of analogies, that involuntary perception even when keyed into a circuit doesn't get looked at moment by moment. Almost a temptation to snatch back, but the city can't identify, its structures are enclosed against it, its ease in containing you won't distort what it conceives of as pure derivation.

Unless you're so far in figure to think it doesn't embody you, you know how to hate it, in which case you become again skinny representation, an abstract service to others, the little mechanic inside the swivelling panel of tricks. It'll have grown stale, yes. Blurring the desire for non-proliferation but against nothing more than the sealed circuit of a nucleus. The screen itself is only cross-hatching of other projections functionally blank because occupied in other directions but otherwise identical in substance. It means defeat was always overloaded and never really had room. You're indistinguishable as foreground and background and as identically reabsorb all that can be imaged against you.

City flesh as no more than a deposition of breath, a crystalisation of house-speech. Where there's variable hierarchy surfaces play card games which are fluent enough, with no reeling back from exceptions either. Only interstices, a correctly aligned periphery, could threaten you with being loved into a character, a beginner, provoke you to a change of density.

Bunkers, kiosks, bin-yards, almost contrive just such a change as the standable, the emptiable, but hardly arrive. Nick into walls affixed by some one applicable precision but otherwise slackly derive from the city which, were a little more of it actually on the ground, they'd tend to divert, downtraffic, since they don't inspirit concentration but rather relieve it. Parked in the city's waiting-zones they're whatever haze it has, a decongestant also were the city not brittle with oversight, having always just that inclination to groove-jump.

Enclosures are unreliable though about the textures of cities which they tend to generalise. They don't understand difficulties of finish, that the city's most itself when it struggles with outskirts it daren't relinquish, doesn't know how to make peripheral. Which stay around with full equipment, called up via corner-walls and porches, the partitions chalky, paths continuous but less than direct between low horizontal ridges which divide but don't allow the outskirts to die away. Streets open onto further beckoning channels perhaps neighbours but not indications, the only geography the city attends to is you're still in it. But not room capacity, rather a cellular mud which continues to ooze, welling into water where the drip foliates across horizontal thrust. Having a lively abundance of flapping interruptions, fairweather hauls, slanted fences and hoardings rigged bermuda, the partial lakes amuse appreciative pockets of locality which not only prevent any wide sweep of view but undulate under the feet, small steady currents sway the centre-board into oblique possession, the house-hunt to begin round the inner side of the door.

The houses reflect the city in use, lending hands across surfaces not preventively steep, anticipate and elicit it, always between deaths and removals in a state of make-ready. But the earth long become choppy and granular with repeated occupation seems to nestle structures having a lean-to effect as if dependent on some inapposite principle of shelter, squatting along the edges of boundary features, memorizing ditches as if they too might become tenderly derivative, provincialised by some rift descended from landscape which now does little more than peer stilt-like down parkways. But once the nexus of the old locale is tapped, corked (a tender substance), expansion is exactly less the old resistance, boundaries that still communicate some bias of surface become the city's underworld attracting outfilling, wide-splayed pith. The city's a seepage of ringways, perforations that never feel sufficiently enclosed alarm further lining to cosset every outer edge, downy nearest the air of periphery: warm air as the city tenderizes itself by surrounding itself one more round, too many embankments where the circulation of inner and outer is truncated by access to every trial of greening.

Description is part of the bias that accords so much more structural liberty to leaf-texture.

Comfort is to feel itself perceived in tight-lipped beams which it's urbanely distending, is brisk with operation then, smartly interchangeable, begins to yearn to overhang landscape or have it delve in a little once a pan of comprehensive vision is assured. Resistance at the periphery confirms the equability of encirclement, suburbs display a disingenuous facility for space. As it's all for pulling back into the eye of centre whose beams fuse the paunch of implant rather than cauterise.

The sectors align and correct shadow to the extent they're radial, renewable, not directly grounded or long-grained in imitation of underlying fibres but leaning into narrow incisions only so far as to jump between parallels, exchange surfaces after a limited pursuit. Where shelter evaporates in the train-compartment always entering it, snug enough under a pool of reading-light but on some other schedule empty and directionless (at an unmentionable after-journey which is the city's functional periphery), suspended over sharp threads of sidings where ground is irrecoverable, the partitions overdrawn from the warmth of passage.

The city's about to become central far more deeply than an appeal to intensity, to offer how promise is final, a sudden layer to feel wild over, an encased nucleus role-perfect, defective resolution over one pole too nostalgically written off by the other to balance out the information, know-how stranded in the preliminary field of operation, the outlying having been too much dragged into the explanation. It might yet conjure low pressure round it, ballast the asymmetry of centre with compensating norms, the amenable natural, but its conventions stay closed against it. In the enclosure.

To decentre the city, make mat the luminous nucleus, absorb in roughcast the screenless eye within an enclosing periphery (which being peripheral may darken without formality) isn't only to misplace the city's inventions but to be humoured by invitation. The city pursues with familiarity, is the originator of its own reject-tissue which already perfectly endures your replacement-zone where you oscillate alongside flickering ambulances. Desire for periphery must bear with the falling limp of the centre of its idea, and with alienation already far advanced into another brand of easing up: the tension between alternative rooms which dazzle themselves with the not yet inhabited, cluster on the same level taut with private insights into ulterior decorations of inclusion/exclusion which promise to instate the centre, a built hierarchy in a landscape of a simpler sum than the ground available. The city awakens stranded by what won't leave it out because it can now be managed every time, your choice more used to it than you are. Loosening up on general advantage and pair out.

6

Whether anything about on the road or not. Interruption endlessly reduces to urbanisation.

I'm only crossing which enclosures can well tolerate, running as they do clean up to verges kept weed-free in shadow, protean lead-by boundaried in tall surmise. Crossing at this point elevates the enclosures' long gradient and sheers the road's tube, the mildness of enclosure candidly insentient in its overarching, moving up outrig to outrig of tall-backed notched trees. Channelling cross-grained in the instant that's precisely the step-up into Slufters, high-lying but concave, a deflective bank downbreasting traffic.

The city's dazzle lies among borders known as well, perhaps to bemuse a continuity that would otherwise be too homogeneous, too potently sheltering—and such a suspended but undeferring centre naturally regulates perception outdoorwards, the nostalgic illuminator appears to originate what it derives from but lets it appear, an image it would gladly remirror returning its origin to a glassy displacement of land, hadn't it that look itself.

Or it may do no more than infill crevices of irreducible periphery almost feckless in being so little convertible, deserving inept handling—the enclosure might barrack it into a little operation but the city perches where it can, keeps its vocabulary overhead. Not finding, not standing, in that sense blameless enough but the city capitalizes its site as a coherence, an eye that remains light-collecting, breezes landscape into euphoria scattering the powder that facilitates road surfaces. Certainly unharmed by any kind of field hate, that kind in particular, by resentment at how easily it breaks down, finalising light incising the scored leavings with broken glass.

Over-reaction registers the asymmetrical centre, the outlandish overview. The city's not for balance or skirting round but for passing through intent on some other place (intention delights it) and waits to be reduced to conjurable system not requiring generosity.

Leaf texture was always a dissolvable partition and entry through it accompanied by the outside in recycle seems now more familiar, one of the city's surfaces, the flickering and needlings of enclosure, a dry river in the topcrests, one of the city's choices. Periphery is attended to but the city underwrites, slipping rubbery plates beneath the wood, not inviting opposition but content with whatever steep variety the embankments grow, these things and leaf litter must pass through a point of surface attachable in its demarcations, a sort of empackaged deliverable soil. The city stands to for what enclosure has to work on, no way of ensuring from that whether or not enclosures derive.

Could we annoy the city less, avoid its disruptive withdrawals (the suburbs are turning back in confusion) and let its inclusiveness actually resonate the back of contours, we might find its revisions aren't much less than the strictness of landscape. It holds us, whether or not in the beginning, there alone we're visible alone, it lights us toward a moon of expanse, complicit extension. Meanwhile, what this site is, wind-rhythms, valvular textures within/without as vegetable constructs, gravel drives encircling and distributing these visitors, cross-reference the city by needing to enclose what departs it, what the city also accompanies: prestructure that refines badly scenting some protective retention.

Is this enclosure or city reserve, the city's roadside access to its own antibody, a place where its conventions feed and swell on a groundedness they can never hope to utilise? Which the soil floor undertakes but at a price of difficult comers, enveloping whom it undulates still several degrees below dazzle but shaky at the vast approach for reparation.

Slufters begins across rising embankment which it fences to ensure, but very thinly, the direction of its descent. The numerous rides are slow to enter, anxious for junctions, visibly anticipate each others' support between stands that don't solidify. Gravel fears its divisible priority like a lack of road-sense abandoned to no good purpose. Inside the enclosure the road seems nearer, beyond the immediate outer brushwood any other will seems slender, or deflected outwards in resistance, there's a thinness having the flatness of reflection, the sheen of a growth inhibitor. The enclosure retains outline, rears up and blots out, but doesn't smother with texture, seems slow to buckle up to effective density, naïve before glaring clearances.

This is Slufters without the tenor of enclosure, less the crispness inviting to a centre announced precipitously at the edges, but disservingly admits to being still in process, for when at last the rides find their way into parallels it's between half-made stands which the outside over-reaches. Poles brush up temporarily, expect some rerouting or trail without depth ready for lifting. Here and there where confidence thickens a little they clearly inhale as verges. Lower down exposure has Slufters not fissuring but simply unready for containment, still knitting, dishevelled by the widelay of hillside it has taken up, translated into itself to be as prematurely translated out of, and hardly a blur between.

There's a treachery of scale in the fluency either side of the fences which echoes the road's transliterating band, a shameless parallelism against which the enclosure hasn't the weight to lean on its borders and replicate the motion its way round, as grain redirected—though still penetrably available and reminiscent.

Embarrassing for enclosure how visibly it has designs on the outside even though not yet fixating—plotting flows that otherwise broaden and become pool-like at a bottom itself headed off and filed to a crease by the tail of Slufters. The isolation of old pines is mimicked by milder but as yet less stable colleges: enclosure as construction. Enclosure as invasion: not a voluntary reseeding of heath country but a precinct sent by the city before itself to homogenize magma it can't convert, a revisionary periphery as sanctuary for dilations otherwise too underlying: a room in which whatever softsistence, pre-outline, pre-occupational, the city expels during the production of room-capacity can be settled round an opaque set of dikes from which no central image returns.

How things get meant, the direction of the distinction hasn't so far been important, a conspiracy of enclosure would come in any case to exactly the same arrival: rounding of the city, encircled projection not itself habitable, the unlived house or the space houses on being entered no longer rely on, but enfolding the lineaments of a house and in all other ways amenable, not about to be lived in, not a history, not an alternative.

Do I expend you in design or contract you whole to follow in your direction? Your sex saved its centre, its symmetry not subject to extension, but is endlessly diffusive at the edges with left-over narrations, and these like the dangling asymmetry of townscape must be gathered without skimping texture, to infold around a strict periphery that isn't a function, not an explanation, to that extent not an evasion. But a respite—this evasion allows.

Slufters imprints landscape, shifts it and comes to suffer the displacements of construction, but its conventions are enclosed within it, its temporality will include freedom from older transformation.

7

Towards Broomy the plain slakes itself, a reservoir within concentric seepages of enclosure accumulated flush in spongy envelopes, but where Broomy serves as end-channel clearing increase, something of a crisp tongue drying out Holly Hatch. In a place of copious intention close on mutual relapse it still keeps an edge not too deftly limited but neither serrated by undergrowths, alert to enough open heath not other trees' border.

Its configuration is likely to set towards—a classic tendency to enjoy the derivations which approach it especially where the paths thin into strict tradition in every other sense obstructive, excerpting no further surprises, no longer cropping between lawns or collecting round pools like water. As enclosure transmitting a steady striation of light freckling more clear stands of poles than any damp underclutch would have it, is immediately recognizable, this far out already in range of that dry light.

Lack of waywardness in meeting the open is confirmed by strangely unspeculative deer which skirt it, pastoral or open-bound, trusting in this approach of mine no less sudden than any other that the intervening brakes are sufficiently uncustomary and framefree not to be crossed/ redrawn, the open that space which is not to be diverted. They empark among human scents which the open can still just defeat, watchful out of Broomy's angle of the eye expansively grazed across enclosure-laid heath.

Inside I'm reminded the friability of texture reaching into the canopy without slackening is what the edges were. Inside draws such rendered edges—nodal but also flush sockets lying within outline, in the puttied depth but brightly tensed, not formless in the sense of skinless but a thoroughly imprinted texture. Oak-struts are closegrown and hung in a myriad of collocations that leave the underlitter a free space not annexed to the effort of rootage.

Outskirts had most visibly captioned the authority of enclosure but it continues now in a seam needing no further demarcation, no further re-entry into the outline of the within, no damp obverse edge of the without: pattern renews shoulder-height, the outlook of the place must have accompanied this filtering through of the place itself, modal walking which in reaching up to the well of each short-boughed tree is evident at ankle and knee.

This is a density which stubs solidarity into uprightness, abjures invasion or further persistence, not intertwining. Pigs root along allowable interstices and find the search-grain even. I follow under ochre light powdering under wide banking—but not layering in any priority of edges—here any wedge of growth as easily borders the rest and the heath-dry selvages out in what the openness is doing are as much bearers of texture.

Not in an extra degree of entering but a sequence tripped at centre. If this is the heart of enclosure, slightly emergent from the spray of plantations and better able to aspirate all that floatage, it's in containing no gradation. The rediscovery of what it might be to be contained, or the discovery of what it might have been to have been, isn't here, isn't enriched by the centre itself—simply a better calling in of paths, drying them into the instance of collection they always dreaded.

The centre as no more than a mention along passage is part of the economy of enclosure, but the moment at which direction finds what it always intended by vacating upheld in a blank suspension of repetition pointing exactly from its own unproviding axis. Exposure of what paths always sought making too much of itself on the ground, with a risk of becoming less releasable, too easily traceable, an open premeditation on what only a further place was trained to enjoy as if the further place had come too soon or its postponements reverted into sudden over-actual admittance.

But not retaining. Silence beyond enclosure is as amenable as the permitted mention of entry, what won't extend is as much release of the outside ahead as compaction of the outside behind. The enclosure's only narrow about ways round, blocking a wider freedom from development, insisting on this one admission, that its non-transformation is for walking through.

The centre won't stay, falls into difficult use once only and rather than undermine the path's deferred embodiment by so deeply containing it, empties itself as if also in pursuit. Enclosure's standing across is over-literal, an overdrive of sequence I never thought to have gathered in dis-closure, and meeting it here won't have disclosed. Not repeatable except the sequence will have gone on, no furtherance except in the pressureless gel of the outside.

No outline except infolding what needn't stay within boundaries. Vitality bounding unlinked poles suddenly dropping through a well of membraneous closure, the walking muscles willowy in reach-up. How, rather than any uncompromising frame at ground level, enclosure ensures it's non-disruptive. Priority of texture over form that would otherwise only immerse in a repetition of frames.

Edges, as a convention assimilated and allowed continued operation, are stark only through an immediate matness, a platform of location not further illuminated, a point of non-proleptic containment (however the paths lean into emptying) immanently not detaining. Wholeness as something other than endlessly deferring openness or even astringent over-againstness. Enclosure in its nest of palings edged-through seems to compact landscape into walkable density by ditching and incising, but the edges too need to enter, to pass through, vanishing as surfaces into the energy of singed grain, infrastructural heat, the fire-risk injected into what goes no further. Not going further is equally relative, this local absolute is as if burnt to a local direction, a singular quantum not overarching. Enclosure as limitation of the significance to be attached to enclosures—in that sense especially a non-clearance of boundaries.

The other side of which isn't emergence, or at least no exit with fresh conventions—deferred perhaps by the post-immediate presence of centre.

The whole habit is one of passing out within direction or hierarchy, the enclosure too little flawed to loiter round its visibility or gaze at what the trees conform across what might equally well be a fallen tree. The path empties out at a mortise of embankment long muddied away leaving only wide frameless extraction into a sky again proportional to the outside.

Splash Bridge is as much a derivation of classic enclosure which it services without being offered shelter. Emergence would characterise shelter from what?—no more is sheltered than the sheltering part: enclosure which didn't disparage passing interest prevented love seeping into an ungrounded closeness, crystallizing in a collective ring dazzling the uncrossed matness lying between which even the idea of absence makes too simultaneous. No periphery to be taken for an exchangeable context, it's not to be confused with urban interpenetration either, but as an inhibitor alone retaining the difficulty of where you are: that part of myself in you no longer present to itself you no longer represent.

At Splash Bridge the path laps dust, plies a bleached quilty sand, its stones pushed deep by hooves under the powder. Self-sown pines border the enclosure's breakwater and take the powder upward. Over by Sloden's low ramble no connecting path is visible which gorse roughcasts as the stems of trees.

Love not going further isn't reusable except in desire for a compensating idea to be absorbed in its time, not having ceased, but with insistent local edges (the body's matness) not continuable either. Love is a favour making little room for its idea, so tautly inhabited its resonances appear no further—except at the periphery with benefit of a little slackness. Preventing the loss of description.

On a stump neither here nor Sloden's, or in a gorse-brake the stump alone identifies, a stonechat dries its watery cover into air, rubs its dry chee round this dropped hub of landscape not in love, the last avail of love not plummeting in a place, the one eliminable by the other as sky and water are without the least priority. Pebble-smooth, liquid or dry, what is there for either ground to render other than the rub of two invocations being audible?

8

Hasley is less enterable, the heath specifically takes care. Goes beyond dust-level where a haze of texture would have needed outlining by walking through, on over a surface of aerated stones up a path much blustered clear, clinching the position with a lessening need for arrival. The enclosure is already met with, taken to without reserving entrance and becomes less enterable. On the path flints split through directions already covered.

Erection of shelter in outward guise straight up at the outside with all exposure granted. The toptrees of parent firs signal how much the outside can be let take off what it can, ragged masts with easy separations screen as much prime location as they like onto their own seedlings but refine very little else in terms of closure, bind room only for future tallness. Such beacons remind at once that similar identification is possible from the Hampton Ridge side simply by switching channel within the same band of signals. The enclosure has become like its journey, less of a transfix on the immediate path—it's questionable whether to use the path through it at all or skirt on any track round what seems to want to intend identical flanks. A hangar. Already something of a post-complete erasure of the workings of enclosure—though not a revision—simply less doing at familiar curt economy.

Leaving enclosure is a way of omitting the approaching one. Emergence is itself tactful landscape, a visible location not needing the involution of preliminary entrance just to be sure of coming out right. Exit simply takes Hasley straight as sufficient demonstration not needing to be acted out, not a matter of being accompanied by commentary from yet more quitted embankments. The rails ahead stay ahead, demarcating a shelter enclosure no longer has to prepare, the cover no longer exactly simultaneous.

Exit as sufficient idea, an after-effect bent on imaging backnumbers of its own schedule, a post-positional concept hoping to prove enclosure was one way of not always having been one but a containment before a theme emerged. The abstraction isn't regained by walking through repeatedly, its idea of origin may have worked exactly, but having sewn up the prestructure until a coherent idea broke over it emerges now as an after-idea.

It's no less direct to skirt the ridge on which Hasley so deliberately departs, and peer through into bunches of chestnut poles divided by what is sufficiently idealising the interior ride. This much though—Hasley's still for peering into without which the chestnuts don't appear. Exit's from the outside but from much the same intimacy.

Having been contained, not having stopped despite the place being no further, not having resented continuation beyond whatever stoppage seemed to be on the point of inventing—the whole reaching a stage of advertisement—must be internalised now. Otherwise containment has a way of not exemplifying the within.

This encampment on the last rise before the northern ridges, abrupt post planted by those who already had an image of enclosure, seems framed into outlying reception, perfectly obtainable before I can be brushed or shadowed into it. Not that going in is absolutely forbidden—but the effect's already out here in the emergence. Enclosure as reusable idea isn't had by keeping inside but comes as the first prompting of a finitude that's closed over, after which it's tactless to refuse uncharacteristic consequences or fail to see what might have been so described can no longer be so contained. I can only admit its surfaces preferred to deal reversibly despite all.

The effort of walking rises to an airiness of the ahead no longer in sequence with the journey. The journey is to wherever the unearned is. Enclosure to apply shouldn't have been knowable but is certain to be now, and as an idea about its application. Its unity does have to be represented, the fact it was never able to be interrupted is where exit remembers.

Stepping through a part of it wasn't to block off that part but on the contrary internalise the whole visible ringstop, the lost segment collecting a fluent circuit of blockage. I'm outside the prodding weather of the about-to-be-completed now, but equally, with the same exposure to weather, outside what has been completed. Walking isn't opaque anymore, its idea of where it's been can only be asymmetrical, projected at a driving edge. As though enclosures being grounded wouldn't turn back as absences, being concretised equations into which I could steal to make just one rooted terminal present, wouldn't evade, wouldn't be able to have moved on.

In not moving on they flitted into the after-impression of support, an idea formally incompletable. Only in the determinate weight of that sort of wrong arrival does anything like the seizure of enclosures remain.

Enclosures always had that fault, the necessity to be thought round, and though needing in the end to be assimilated to more than their own opaqueness were only ever able to attract into themselves the ascriptive light of the plain by virtue of their own prior coherence.

Centre doesn't delay the centre and wouldn't, did it, stay there. An idea no-further continues intentionally, its source of retention demands exercise, quartering itself, taking a turn beside its own partial instances. The idea of enclosure is that sifting of totals, always reforming as it discerns re-entries into the initial unresonant compass, dividing from territorial fixation but in the same occupiable instant repinning, narrating the absorbent centre as that sort of process, earning the carelessness of centre, its innumerable stases.

The difficulty's to place a filled room on an equal footing with an empty one, a difficulty of still creating rooms which aren't required for further containment. The idea, trying to reproduce the dimensionality of space within itself (the get-out), sensing in managing its own exit there's still a roundness left, a round inter-change between relative densities of enclosing objects from the opacity of which it withdraws with the relief of coming after, feels the effort of building such a grid as if it could be challenged to make room for an interstice. As if the empty outside could shame it away from infilling towards a mutuality of equivalences. But the mind solidifies only indirectly, otherwise it's the discrete texture of the head it can hardly enter: on looking back it duplicates the outspread map of the heath through which the invisible wind runs a wire—or on further invention becomes detachable—most into itself when making some such stirring of translation.

Later translation too has an instinct for exit beyond any point where one equivalence nests in another. It's one way for the idea of enclosure to lose its centrism, but not being able to soften boundaries indefinitely is still hornily nucleated, still circling reflection.

The finitude of enclosure leads to abstract evacuation (the abstraction operates). Is there anything which could still be reoffered? Any involute homing-in through the lost stretch outwards, a dissolute centre as the readable edge of diffuse extension?

Still the commonplace of separation, a dualism on the ground I could always recognise by as much as three sides but the fourth I couldn't intend, that exit-row of palings is blank, a flank by which the idea of enclosure is itself detained, a border into the named other returned to only by the other name, a collusion that managed neither possession nor conversion though starting from the same nominal preliminaries as the self.

Whitefield Plantation is from here thoroughly experienced at being pared down, a clump on the edge of the Perambulation visualizing its own distance and solipsistically putting itself there. As such trackless, continuously fenced but without secrecy, barely a double row of sightable trees not divisible into an arresting idea or of hardly enough mat dross to be divided from one, not simply proposing the unenterable but unlikely to be walked near. A calendar mark of the periphery with a recurring lack of reference.

Hasley became oddly blunt once skirted and a perfectly life-like path leapt out of it at the last, but Whitefield's a site-screen, a last thin obstructive brilliance allaying what featurelessness might tread the heath through the windows of a pivotal country house. Emparkment plants a paralytic representation of enclosure to give grounded resistance to the hollowness of the authentic idea of one.

But if plantations were really once a blockage convention they won't stop chattering over the shoulder of the open now, the shapeless follow-on discovering just after closure the vital explanation they defeated but which becomes now their prolifically inventive voice. There's nowhere after all for which enclosures are the wrong place, where their clarity wouldn't be assertively left over. By which nature's representable, thematically concerned for what love furnishes, equipping with space, interpreting enclosures as coherent again in the play their interferences reinvent: a room of one's own in the convention of prior coherence. Love is a retrospective gesture about original sealedness from which love may yet gain though still as pursuing a union not quite on centre. Love the intentional traveller was unable to relieve asymmetry.

How is it I love you unconditionally when I only arrived through the immaculate condition you owe? It was that which closed over you into an illumination of sources, post-positional brightness. But now true to say it, you're loved for your own beginning. This prolific lateness is what origins are yet to touch once only, a beginning to the lateness of the metaphor.

This tightening of space from which love has a habit of beginning sees now where/against what it gathers. There's a hollowness of still more receptivity conjured from the mat centre of the emplacement. The hollowness can be a threat at any moment, but equally, being fixated in over-representation, may return again at any moment to the simplicity of landscape. Enclosure was that opaqueness yet to be outlined but imagined as absorption around precise lockgates of assimilation, and becomes now in such an exit inverse internalisation, an openness without entrances, an opacity subsequently filmed round the accretions of love.

9

Broadly no longer between enclosures, no longer in that wake, the plain solves its continuity. Nothing prevents winding openly beyond plantations withdrawn into low gorse grubbing the edges of skyline. Ibsley Common having the space it wants has it out here clearly not interrupted by the stresscounts of trees. It's not to be sensed into underlying direction but has no natural genius either to disallow a track wandering up one if a notch in the skyline seemed for a moment isolatable. It's long breasted what it will, no need to disavow making a deadline over trenches earlier ruts perhaps along some equally unremoved way.

Sky has to be included as the appropriate encounter, constant untyings have become constituent here. Even overhead where young black cattle feed down dried-out gutters it doesn't make a concave pinned to the plantations flickering like nettles under the sills of the plain, but is the only possible neighbour: the other unbroken plateau easily debited to passing events, plumped out by cloud formations or strung through the flight of an engine hum. It has its own undeferred additions not as reactions to the underhand, contractions mirroring the Common into whereabouts, but as simply what the Common out of enfeebled derivation is likely to be exposed to. Itself also the same contingent exposure, similarly lacking any gradation of distance and with the same much influenced texture. Intimacy as a vein heedless of detail.

Structure's a vestige here, the Common hasn't escaped it but isn't vitally undergoing it. Form has it but finds itself laid wide somewhere, initiative adrift. But can be tolerated just as the enclosed route here likely to have overmanaged form can also be. The Common's inattentive to modes of access even where they intend to continue influence. A sort of landing won't implicate an ungathered tangent, its outboard closeness. It feels like nearness when Ibsley lets slide even a peripheral frame, isn't visible care: remaining what incises under the spawning heel, as a texture not to be condensed by striding over.

Were enclosures the real interstices, but cunningly decoying all this broadness impossible to avoid? It would have come out to as much for the whole landscape, but via this approach enclosures' high-density, the sleek entrance chutes, seemed the obvious way round promising to cope with any halflights left over. Not that Ibsley's out to make difficulties other than being continuous into Rockford by a minor road: dips are sharable rather than toplands separable, and the gravel pits not appearing till the last moment aren't hierarchical, rather a fall off the scale of density altogether—as inverts scarcely divide.

It's strange how the Common seems to lack any sense of intrusion or any of the obscurity of that lack. Roads, trees, hutshells, or the newish communication armlets which are anything but local, don't establish more immediate networks or alternative perspectives. The Common isn't a centre though possibly an arena, a swathe of no longer narrowly drifting space which it would be trite to invite much else to take a hand in. The perceptual locale no longer mutates.

Isn't simply where enclosures come down to though, a downstream site after the formalities of exit. Enclosures lie obliquely here, leaving-off not particularly unconditional in a place not necessary to be beside. But the outside they interpreted might at least be taking itself literally. Space has a use for hierarchical operations but an odd way of laying out each occasion, seeming to suspend each function along each moment in what becomes eventually a lack of pressure, though in no way lessening walking through as unavoidable carrying of place.

Enclosed suggestions scud across the Common, still onto something, occupational, trenching for aptitude. The Common hasn't anything by which to oppose them except to angle shafts of conditionality and unconditionality as both equal exposures it's likely to look straight into. Not that enclosure's unbecoming as a side-feature. Wasn't it frontality that from the first wanted to be reoffered? I'd hoped for evidence of recompense like a gaze which had turned away?

Enclosure, a buoy concealing dimensional mastery below the water-line, hardly endures focus now, bobbing not very amiably on the surface. It'll trail the Common on a retrospective basis across a length of plain that isn't interested in betrayals, a level hinterland trawling perspectives it has no intention in combining. Not here contingent location bothers to claim a flatness more authentic than the drained surround of plantations. The Common beckons the tact of enclosure whereby desperation isn't morbidly inclusive but displayable alongside. Interferences enclosure characteristically refuses to count internal, reserving them on lateral heathland that might relieve it of the irony of competent containment.

Having already let the not-entered be closed off, condensation of what didn't enter. It was where the plot was likely to have kept in bounds, be about something there, but its damaged mode made excessive grounding necessary, anticipating the event and practising the aftermath of what love was still unexpectedly to choose. Now ragged opening, entangled self-hollowing leaking into the eye of the plain, the only coherence something about the way an enclosure craters, spiralling its abnegation round a turntable, the ringstop, the idea of not inventing for ever, challenging the plain in case it became only farther order.

But the neighbourhood in which to practise whatever restraint enclosure could have devised, a parallel turning from upward and outward dreams, the resentments they describe, and absence, including the absences in the description. Enclosure is that long side-look too continuous to subvert. The skirting round of love in evasive self-reparation to be comforted in wider landscape is what the outside always was, free-wheeling evasion blowing laddered rooms too fresh to get stuck there—the open I thought I wanted after the heretical climb, too exposed, the Common and the sky, for confrontation. The ease of knowing how to undermine the self was an illumination the matness of enclosure always avoided.

From here it might be enclosures never very ably entombed their own kind of apparition after all—a regression interpreting them could all too easily slide towards now. It's more important to have anxiously recognized them having landscape options. The trail of compulsive walking through remains, not falsely outlined as such—rather enclosure was a way of distinguishing experiences not themselves containable but the priority of any specific falling into, the detail eventually taking over the goal of origin, never simply netting it like a hold-all but as a dread making beginning intrusively where to begin. The gesture's not reversible now, a hierarchy has thought of strenuous arrival.

Alongside which are companionable commons. Easily the place, open, broad enough, where emptiness of chest, uncertain movements of wrist and knee, can appear as things hoping to be re-enclosed—but reckoning without the economy of enclosure. Containment's less than inclusive while it has its own production to attend to. Nevertheless parading factors which inhibit love, the romance of being less lovable in extravagant faith to what may be found out so that love in wanting to rejoice as infallibly rejects. I might have wanted love to contain it all, including trips to lessen it, but love out of respect for resistance narrows the proprieties of rescue. The unconditional's only one of several plains out here. Love may be chary of recording distances first laid down in mild encounters as if they were space but can't help grounding the obstruction in a vale of adoptions too, since it's such a gratuitous originator.

It's projective in that way, ontologically it's jutting through, but the suffered awning ensures the limits of what it starts from stay on the ground, make contact on return. The distance of another name is prospected if not represented at a time when hope wants invisibility. I need to free you from myself, I threaten you too much in doing it. I can't absolve you from what is for you too a common space. Releasing you is additional meaning you circumscribe—perhaps that was always the effort to uphold enclosure—to desire a ground of possession from which alone release feels better. The silence of giving you back to yourself, the silence of not repeating in you what I was to have become there, isn't going to be affirmed, is constantly negated by willing itself to be, making the unentered clearly distinct again, hoarding you as releasable.

What silence might have tried is siting enclosures so they continue as damaged contractions, displacements adept in the art of place, ravelling up thematic rearrangements which they might make tolerable—suggesting a reserve which appears prethematic, incipient illumination reserved from ever being called on. The modes of place are capable of reappearance through whole cycles of convention and subterfuge, and despite all solidify into something visitable. An emplacement resists transcendence but having absorbed it quite geographically goes on attending to causes and uses, goes on tempting meaning as an embodiment, or that aspect of the loved body which seems non-transferable, non-equational.

Only an exploitation out to set profuse inventions of absence onto mats can be reoffered. Your swarmbeat, bothersome compactive presence, is its possessive inference. It too makes existence claims even when in collusion with failure, evasive opacity what the blocks course as. Otherwise I'd be reduced to the game of never having seen the room. Reoffering you as you might have been on the other side of love reckons without that sleek site, the perspective you're in-sight-of, the place where your image isn't given up but a highly grounded elongation made of it. Merely sensing you'd been there is to have an acting version designed to make it just as grounded to deinterpret, and would have started therefore with an idea of love coming to just such a well-made place to be emptied out. Which of us there ever stayed on the look-out? Instead let the distancing remain as what wants to come a long way from a delayed intimacy, the other way round of the place which the same sight-lines catch, as, inversely, a telescopic corridor advances from its own contraction, as love is the other way round into the body, its unpresentable mutuality.

Though enclosure's no less in the roads of attraction—your non-differentiation of levels of desire, lack of any sudden alternative feature. A harbouring locum parts airily round linear mouths becoming the straight flow-on the Common is, where enclosure might inadvertently have suggested brief over-confirmed ecstasy. Not that levels which elsewhere might have been decisive weren't cued—an eclecticism of houses but hardly suggesting the difficulty of the street, separate windows but all at the view together, none blinded or peering back but needing enclosure to conjure away the breathlessness of delight already in place by the slowest provision of origins.

Attainment was in the fit, love could only be feckless in recognising you were already gained if it cared to equalise the variable of where it was you divided where—not that here/there could be let decline a way into the global. Enclosure could touch you by limiting possibilities, less than its equation once only, counting on absence being for one runthrough a further or similar specification of any attainment, a slowing down of your provenience through loss. Loss hoping to reveal the already arrived as the ground of whatever perspective impinges on you, possession or loss equally late but for a short seizure merciful at post-creation. Your freedom/distinctiveness won't be reoffered so much as this thematic use of you, what you can't but offer of yourself, what you can't be free from, the asking long ago delivering over(this is it into this) in which you too were bound to intrude with the same common delay your own arrival.

Words that overhang the method, arch between sex and landscape, keep abroad by germinating in the hollow connective excitement, keep the interstice inhabitable, find analogies to fray in a repetition of desire what alone steals the confusion: a rooted interruption forever believing in it re-enacts, finds itself an alibi for structures of justification, its insistence on not benefitting from its own discredit indistinguishable from collusion. As if to advertise, what is it waits for the settling of boundaries, for the trap to solidify, in the paralysis becomes a little distinguishable which without disturbing the seamless body underpins the way you've been loved?

10

To the direction of Appleslade—to the notch in the skyline magnetically nominal, a half-encumbered circus scrawled illustratively against glaze of the enclosure belt. A daub finally stumbles over image and squats on a lump freer and more revisitable than the rest of the mass. Not continuing the small road that named two Commons on either hand, but would lead back now into the full gleam of Milkham and Slufters, but turning down the side of whatever path derives Appleslade.

It's a strange plantation, ripe in the description overhanging a garden smelling of already seasoned fruit—but that would be more a property of the house, and Appleslade is more of its name than a veritable storeyard of enclosure.

It's a way of revisiting names reminded by a different name. Seasoning the taste but constantly hovering on the lee of approach rather than needing to be set firmly into boundaries. But always well thought of, the hope of what enclosure gives to take away. Appleslade occurs mostly outside palings as a style of the inside promising to wait for the outside. Like looking down into the dell where larch and spruce descend the mossrun most invitingly, and having no possible path between them the invitation must be one of level-sharing, of a reconciled elevation cupboarding the head.

From Appleslade less euphoria—or possibly not the right names accompany. Back to skirting enclosures continuously again until another road is reached towards which even the little track coming up to Highwood is too elaborate. But as it is one of Appleslade's embankments isn't justified by heath but bolts into woodland, into the tangent of Red Shoot—the first named wood, rich continuous oakland and holly, probably never enclosed and even now too dense to have any sense of its own intervening. How does enclosure do it when up against an outside of equal density, one that doesn't threaten with inflow but prevents a vacuum cabling the plantation's fences—the ring of low pressure into which it can refract a closure-signal and pan back, enveloped in a trough of minimal resistance by which it countermands its own overarching? Not that Red Shoot is severely close-grown. A lot lies easy at ground level in canopy breaks where fern and holly aren't immediately distinguishable. Animal paths root through each section of the wood that needs to be worked over and fed from, none imperative, none directionless. Crinkled borders when encountered aren't an event but a passing, though the wood's turgid enough, benched by hawthorn, tubed exactly to its own standing pressure.

Into the triangular headbay of Linford Brook where a cliff of enclosure reappears, making a head into which the water lessens and darkens beside which a blond remade forest track only keeps light through width. But possible to avoid all that and sidle down another way crossing the water almost continuously to take in Pinnick wood with the back to enclosure or the water flowing forward. This isn't open heath through which water clacks but a sky-hole, a cloud-station, one edge hooded and mounted by Roe which leads more that it's willowy, the other two merging into a crabby apex of similar density which ought to represent, if opposed to enclosure, something less possessed. Unless the open was after all always the same pressure, simply a housing differently interpreted? What is it to go from enclosure to cover, from shelter to canopy, from hierarchy to the unequal terraces of Red Shoot? No emergence except into equivalents and by means of holes and gaps which all the terms, not so equivocally, support between them.

Direct foraging into Pinnick with the oaks if anything finer and pollarded beech unfolded—swept more by old axe-habits than as now by wind—and it's here in the late autumn afternoon a sun-wheeled corona of edges (after so much understanding) will have again stunned and liquefied.

It's odd that Pinnick, almost stolen into, should so sufficiently heal its edges, radiant almost the whole way round what the internal snood of foliage delimits. Edges register from where the centre calls no further outlet, an acceptance of installation which light forecasts, not owing continuance. What gets humped around until detachably arrived into. The centre undermines long walked totals of revision by lying diagonally across what's still the first step of departure, no longer portable. The afterlight's no longer internalisable, not understood since here it can be visited again. The centre abides the fixation as a problem of place due to connect what may be lateish autumn light with what (being horizontal) is unfleeting. Flaming non-accumulative though.

Or not accountable. Though the wood bivouacs its own image from within, I remember it more externally still as part of a walk which must have set the opposite direction, to have come from the dual-carriageway (not even potentially near having become thematically redundant) or before that from all the clad distance of Berry Beeches as a way of not having started through Oakley at all, or having deviated but not at the time having accumulated enough walking for Pinnick to become obvious after-effect.

It was some other beginning or quasi-elementary stage rather than the finishing it eventually means. Only after walking is there anything other than arbitrary itinerary from which having walked what wasn't walked over this way is constructed fully the way round. It's the point of the already arrived.

Piercing out onto Marrowbones Hill the sound of the last mentionable place is verified not as an idea of suture but as an idea of having walked its bed of structure alone terminably repeating the ending. Marrowbones, out of the wood but not relevant to the road, under a late September but still blue-domed sky, is much more normal, the sort of place read about, hardly orientating, a mound of foxways and alternating sunbeams that immediately relax their spectacular hub of collocations by which I might have come or got away. An effortless untested hierarchy by which to kite fresh air over roomish trees and find the unavid openness the best gesture of leaving off.

It's not much more than nominal, but having rested I came across its convenience here, learnt to bait it for not being as derivatively sole-sore as other indicators (the sense in which feet chiefly mimic), learnt to pull the name of it through its journeying priority. Words will have to be content with not having walked from start to finish, with having been marketed within the wicker of an athletically itinerant head, the sort outdoor muscles attach to: the sense in which the skull rather than the mind acknowledges the pressure of containment walking limbs uprear.

Other settings-out might have been learnt as muddles, but even if the beginning didn't happen until after leaving the bus (a convention of urban approach not necessarily underwritten), or if having the mistaken the map the makeup of the way was invaded just as wisely, these wandering logistics aren't necessarily any more informal. Each moment of walking imposes a hindrance, its inserted and subversively unmodifiable droplet which words read as a curve into ubiquitous relations, for them what a journey always was. As if having been wound up it could be more amenably fragmented. As if weariness on the ground had made this, if abstraction could be tired into a genuine interstice.

A normal place to get the threat of creation back into some sort of homogeneity as what it can itself say. To talk about a site where you didn't all happen by reference to enclosed spaces where it couldn't but all happen. If you're that other not addressing yourself as that, I wanted to get out there with you as what I don't call myself either. Meaning some bracketed form, realistically lendable place what might appease the prescriptive self, its bridgeless imperative to be on its way into form—but can't abide a process anything less than the already arrived.

All of which is already conjured away preparing to be unlikeable, the trial of the theme of enclosure a last time, what's likely to have the last word over any explicit need for emergence. Is there still some way of getting it here, some smack of place not attended to—since it couldn't after all merge the itinerary with its own know-how? The notation will insist on being another occasion and walking on over revealed ground.

But landscape too had to be wrenched out of absence to frame what was becoming too much the present modification. It wasn't so much you weren't there, I had to harrow a context to justify the lesser alarm of your being close, hope to be at ease enough to set up a periphery hierarchical and attractive but which wouldn't distribute, would fixate as an encumbrance. The unsuitable background, the back-off, would be rejected, re-offered. I must have hoped it would appear a sort of function, though quite futile to deflect you since you remain its centre not drawn out or reflected against. In you anxiety's indicative, almost, when you don't budge, problem-solving.

Landscape looked better on its own but knew that though it never took to love it could never return either to what had left it untouched. That was the gesture humiliation wanted to throw in, to make a fool of itself burning out the obviously specious addition, to have made a fool of itself earning a ground of recompense. Nature taking itself for such a convention lessened itself as if generous only via prestructure and was embarrassing. So it was a matter of using you profusely again to shame the landscape you'd so offended into a series of enclosed forms where its upkeep could again be a refusal to supply.

What are we grubbing at in the country of enclosures? This territory, still the only one which indents, isn't habitual anymore, no longer near enough to supervise other studies, can't surpass its opaque complements except through a further principle of enclosure. And I'm not offering myself that. The terms must stick, some other improvement would be diffusion. Gratefully undertaken though, since it was nothing less than the Perambulation itself rounding up into a prospect of city playground, park-like décor, but still dense enough to be able to reinterpret its boundaries—that means get to them in time, reroute overwhelming urban entrances, a city requiring extraction, to envale availability. It was a contraction tender enough to make me wander whether *it* wasn't the loss, since none of us could follow where it kept us safe. Which was to assign you as a preemptive landscape term, a way or rewearing it, bringing endless density and heathwhiff into a small stub or collar, a reproachable entrance. The other side of which would be strictly unpresentable, no down-through-and-out, yet for all that a distinction we're driving towards. Between-us-as where you're a gesture reverting to its country. To use you to make up landscape was a way of flushing out its variables, traducing you as evenly as possible. Against which, hoping to forget the danger of it being you had another reversal to forget with.

You're not to read that way. It's not that I don't mean it yours but you're not here to read it which is a priority you'll always amend and stay for: the release I envy, to have the sort of absence which kicks at the floor or isn't here because of the rules of the floor. Your absence isn't much bigger than you are. But it's difficult for us not to make some use of the mutuality of the inessential, sufficiently derivative beings to be amateurish impediments to the arcs passing through us (as if we were not and able to wish we were not) which mark us and ground us where we stand nothing with which to resist. You're no more enclosed than I am because the interstice between us is wilful: the centre-as-other not as cheated presence but as a genuine constriction feels like what the centre always was, upgrading the vanishing of the available.

Post-centre was no guarantee of transformation, especially when it wished to defend itself by remaining always on the ground. Love probably works in some other way, the tenderness interminably inhaled can only be guessed at as an analogy for what had already arrived. The whole point of the interstice is that I didn't know whether I risked you lovable or not, and wanted that to matter, even though if you weren't lovable in my way you'd as easily arrive into some other. But that's an abstraction you proved untestable making it now equally difficult to respect the other.

Love in playing with too many negations always survives. Not knowing whether I possess any news in loving you, and if choosing, not wanting to help the person you haven't sent. But even if love hoped to downgrade in context it wouldn't be able to remember itself as such, as having drawn its offence from the concrete. It's not that writing's avoidable transcendence but what remembering won't void that ends as a form of rewriting.

If you're the origin of this. But nothing here depends since your presence never appears, concretion's your own affair. Which is to welcome a projection based on your direction or since I come from that direction, something you must simply hold onto at source while all this keels into the effort of making good the source. Eventually unexposable since your not being here is the far more primary evasion.

Fear of distortion was usually a shift from illegible depth to the only air, where enclosure's that defensible surface from which nothing inhales any higher. Explanations only ever rooted down a little and finding the abandoned surface a surprisingly irrigated elevation made that the ascendant justification. With or without earthworks we peak as far as the ontological plain.

It was safer for the mind to go on imaging that collation in mid-air so that its own reach can appear textureless, over-mirrored rootage that feels unretentive, a room grainlessly slipping from its platform of origin. Certainly at times it'll offload the floating trueform, its impossible openness, by means of conventions of spatial ditching or habitable places, so long as these too have an air of disappearance.

There's no easy access to the flatness of the plain, hard-earned goads of diminishment, especially when pocked every time by crystallizations of enclosure which tend to recur foolishly in a web of gratuitous but reducible origins. Reduction has its opaque tag shelving just enough belonging as not this much further, which, since it doesn't circulate, simply fixates the barrier's sort, the seaming career, of joys.

PROSE WOODS

1985

I PASS WOODS

Roots incite surface, the site got over by woods. The trees as uprooter wend by level of support to universal cover. Of surface excess to near lattice ideal. First induced of us when, subjacent, filters will be fillers. From highly reflective ground (water) to non-reflective crown.

Between sky and tree, cover is the only earth grown out there is. The ground lies in splinters. The wood steps on the ground. From steps of the canopy each nearest neighbour stands.

Regards forward (each head) but no specific pathway since the canopy is without frontal plane. The lateral sluggishness of culture grows upward as between its loads put on, defective-speculative onto the shrug-light of naturalism from among a finish of rims, rind before intent. The shelter-value of rigid lift only thus exposes itself to relish, source above save-all of input.

A rack of uprights the unmarked chance of cover over any rift which did not there spurge it, so to immediate perfect totals over, the canopy over all others' surplus. If the original cradle of impact was local, the crush is spherical now.

A store of sizeable signal, variety of command not yet against. The world curves with overlay, the totality of invasion will be leached out in further union, the cover to be tidal, nasal, printing off an ejector grid. Post-complete (the uprights cross) releases a tensile shielding but into newer veneers, slimmer creams. The repetition a comforter with a fringe of turbulence wherever the whole warmth again was what it goes between, at the overlap gate. Genetic placidity it must resteep to a lattice profusion, unstable equilibrium to acculturate. The asymptote easts among horizons but the canopy casts up shade.

There is only the surface to speculate, upon drift, upon cover, upon cleft, the opining densities: cleft allows cover, follows it to where its failure does not spurn detail. Each foliant is leaching-specific.

Only at such pointing (scoured) can the drop below surplus (the dwelling) imbue integral cover, "that the surface doesn't come without it". Global success must be scratched up before it provides, a safety of volume wheeled over marks of external undercut. Correlate flows with the gouge, already busy at ceiling, the salves.

This is desert to work from, the insoluble monolayer of pinnings-to. The earth returns layer for layer, planning each friction that the tree *is* vertical, in each to its corner. A matter of pricks is any glade we see, spoil-like, goal-like, not untouched but ascending in wreath.

Slender veers, flexible dentristry sent at wind covers, the coating a canal. Flotation of the ball part tipped in acid (the ascendant spines) makes severe wood outline the rotation, the map dignifying global exposure under weather. So much fitted to it damages origin for gain (the shelter): value to partial reserve, a radius to getting amongst, disparted.

Interrupted rampancy is the beginning of an upright ecology. Of surface excess to fractionality, steps without egress. Though the roots by this second completion no longer correspond. Forest decisions do get distributed part by part, vertical consilience is horizontal mesh. The push is simply whatever to the flank solicits cover, assiduously begins signalling any pip past desert as the forest edge (colourful berries, any edge of hedge) will fire across habitat.

Light absorbed sublateral sites para-add: food *is* subversive, the nutrient badges pin up reagent threads. The trees admit they don't retain that, that they had no strict families under roots of their own. Light reflected swords a mosaic of component circulation. Affords coloured bark, intercedes, the weather is after all the bravest formative. Selective crushing, the juices harden skyward. Not to jump such a spot would be continuous, not inquiring, path. From foliar burn to sleeker blow-down.

From finality (a surface grade splits off just that part of itself in species) to intensification (the wavering cradle). Becomes a gallery that can do something about all connections having closed over, revive interest from point to point, origins alike, until we only bend *with* the local, some linkage not accumulating. And command affection for pockets of redisposition once the underbrush is dethroned and heterogenous to traffic. At last accountable openings present themselves standing into the odds where ground has already abated.

Whose business the trees do is decided on standpoint. The light of a needle on a face, the face draws in hand the edge, strolls collective between. Descending from its spherical amount to an ethicality of landscape, choice breaks with fruitable spenders. Inverse grain lattices reverse grain. Retention in the house from the running copse. Fringes moments of shelter after this descent from such a rapid formation of surface in the overspace. Not least, trees go through that. Keen belts must be a culture to them in the open box of forest recruitment.

No hand in that without covering. No span without piers of surface plug by plug the ramble they then read floor to sky as covert. And that only if one limb of the forest strider has been crushed stepping up. The canopy is single-limb on trees, a sub-tract of each pace hooked back so that we are *joined* to any subsequent design of scratch-away. The one buried limb never detaches now but risks it always under cover, the other projectile conducing upward. As outlimb it rents habitable soil, the patchwork of parted surface remaining thus vertical. Due clearance dives by immediate crush to tempo, backlog before exposure.

To be any passage for all this in moves must be its cover. A new later root to the surpassing of surface but by one limb only, the floor then reduced to passages on which the other buried limb may skate. The plenary in leaching back in any case will canalize because we worked folded at immersing each surface before layout overall seemed horizontal, that is (uprightly) was pinned down dry. With moves into demarcation, the free foot scouring.

The free limb detaches its phylum at the extremum only, as a crown wheels root, not round an axis but as one round is geared across another. The overlay is keyboard surface, discontinuous to rendering it clothed but filler on the punched sheet.

Black on white where we cannot get enough of it. The limbs are not dendritic except in never occurring together: presurface root, postsurface canopy.

One-limbed/straddled, fixed/vaulting. Where a bout in woods strides out. Linear-engineered, bound by the thin veins of total forest whose circulation among strong saleable props is passively labyrinthine. The stillness of the wood has still that spherical meander but laid tile to tile in local shelter, its profuse overwork arises each fit. Only the passageways repeat at times the forest's hilt, a shudder of uprightness into those convertibles, a term.

Extract-landscape, arranger and nourisher of the forgotten wood fledged on rising rift, where the leaders all bare it, complex edge from hole below, each solemn stone a further variable extractable. Awe begins in this time but woodside was ever underneath it syntactical, and so supports it: thinned and garbled diswooding, the banding, belting, beating. A scaffolding reared to what specialism?

From the aura of those copses what massive rooms open and close, even graceful far too surrounding. One limb to open or close the other though by vertical moves only, the space's moving past reduced to ribbons now, on minimal strips outbedded rope.

Drift is frequently crudely layered, the irritated point (to the crown) of latent energy. Forward articulation naturally becomes more and more ramified. How do we forward through it? Destabilization of surfaces is having it pass through, the space for wending does not, more than that, have to hollow: the crown does not form as the roots do.

The dispersal dust remains suspended but seed-bitten. Trees grow over it, not centering but in lattices it layers. In layers it arises. An ending of surface as its argument prepared, the complete tree concept some persistent guarantor, vertical but as two-storied high forest. Highly reflective ground (water) is superfeatured in nonreflective crown (the surface). The emblem, the ravages, except as between two limbs.

Against foliage it is necessary to stalk in so oblique a fashion. Stems over and over again remove natural prototype, speculation defectively wide: the covertype. Sediments of the world over itself treed, an ancestry steadily cuts ways to hang it by, each plot of woodland discretely high. Serpentine barren, relevant to wedges of cover wormed through distribution platforms by our landscape having a distillery-angle repose of soil.

Introgression latewood. Parent material was always hinting response-surface with method, and opened itself to superficial deposit. Skilfully obtain the hygiene (its wash) of passing through: lingering is branch-rise, passage alone ajuts the covered square.

Pass on as it is done to, go through to the scarification which is punctual woodland never off the board. A decoration, a chest, but all longingly beset on the exact site as it nothing but a request, hunt the screen until re-verted, sideset in each dwelling stain. As much as stood.

The passage through cover, though cover, is serial to the fixed half, but the limb on which you are free to go must be passed over in its wake, the erect flatness of cover. By returns a landscape not opened out; by too far disturbed, it passes. A scarring there intranscendent, here transigent, a mark on the rise of it, cover that all edge. Of one limb to the other it does fuse, uses avoidance. Pass. It would be hygiene if the (thus) absorbed could be suspended in the exposed. The passage-height of cover.

2 PIERCE WOODS

Where the ground is abandoned the trees themselves pierce an indifferent path, strew in equal direction by taking the dead surface up one indignant load higher. A vanishing of flatness, a wave semilocated, an index between soil and fold, no kinship. Invalid in a group offence, wretched to be growing over. As such the wood's pillar error is itself a wandering lane, an acclivity but to turn vagrant its shallow acceptor state, revirtualize, not embed.

Common to the heap, dereliction in woods weeds up as veering of a total ramification reducible to exposure, but by minimum path. Trees versus true levels only as recursion in opening its spines turns back to true versus, the ground in turning over. Pierces the swarm of apex.

Homogeneity of the site strictly disparages the tree, but worn to ground no longer finds insult. The soil's discompounded gloss never repines invasive recess except against a history of tuneless universal paths, running everywhere on rundown. The pursuit is too equal for the reparation, the paths pierced upright as the trees imitate one remove from improvement. But a revoicer, a site gone thin but over woods go sharp. Cover is a defective conversion never undertaken by what the surface means, but wherever surface cannot stay ahead. Forced hangings along the ground's offensive flaws not remannered by squandrous screening, but as much down unmanned submersibles where roots rereckon the ravage of phase as what will also hold to a piercing.

Starvation must end now by how much the trees let their disrelish cycle, via injective stings of undervalue. Wear not apart from dereliction is on the rise, to be worn at a height of rapacious trees. Faintly vertical the wood screens as if all might turn over it, shutter across bows and dip into site. The ascent adds wilderness not important to be back but freshly germed to neorubbish, fans, sleeves, or dressing adulterate over surfaces which had lain out brilliant too long. That exposure had no other desert for used contours, and the same ground must be abandoned every time there has been a clearing to age it. The wood is the harm it is, its pricks will narrow a transcendent grid, the across-court to history is underwood in the twisting of the wood's beams, the trial of light into cover. A warm lay-up and all scales under the wood pierced uselessly open, insolubly canopied. It is their representamen, their degeneracy loci.

What sinister elasticity all in good covers' part keeps rational how flat it has always been from foundation to gouging out? Trees translate more finitude than there is to raise, take up nothing but cover. Still too high in trees are all snags the ground ever felled, or just where an open-channel chase to multi-daylight amplifies and shreds at the exposure tops. If it is light it is a soft overlay of piercing going on while the wood needles off any broader comb. Limitless layering, arising spokes the more rapidly to disperse exposure, and how sharpened! Axis pierced, stays pierced.

Site renewal ever in readiness beside urban steam but by forest fire turns round to a matting of damage, bonded induration. Useless steps diversely risen to by debris are the latest tree height taken from the air by debris, the seed face perching under smoke will drop the same lattice down, from surfacelessness to cover. Such small trees are the ladder fuels, heterotrophic to slaked earth but alert to slaked air.

Recovery is the grateful reduct of suspension, discharge to seed on discharge alike in drift, and every surrounding industrial floor expects this difference. What is leached at ground veins again the air and wrongs it. Floating shade but non-standard ties, a canopy crossing the bar, air to air not purified but pierced by above-ground woods. And only cover to extend what repulsed solids no longer expect of any surface. But the woods are for it, with deadly accuracy nothing abrades.

Trees reclaim from the ground downwards. Roots in stunning top everything with it. With all channels open the piercing descends through the cleanest groove, what gouge sending for grove always was. Shelterless habitat takes its peak leaves face on, the scar compliance as they fall to litter, as the cycle ascends its classic curve. The scouring has its trees in hand, scrape or cope, what is a dislocation-total on either plane? The drop or the shade, the recovery gulfed by a ceiling binding? Forgotten on all points of piercing any talk of a reserve surface, do the lights not have these lengths easy, all verticals open and excused path?

3 PRESS WOODS

Hills to be thickened over and if with heath abound marshalled by strength of woods. To thinnest upland at floor but overall (the shade) works to this layer too in nothing but the press retains. Finer pressing and wilderness has become in intervals, studies. A potential for roof-culture which permeates, has under-permanent the heath's astrictive zone on surface.

But shadeless cool in closeup to press, almost no offensive overhang. At the heart of the poles the dark is another column of air tallmost shadeless. Tall without height (tallness already lateral-headed), low without loss (loss is ascendant). Where is the forest enough? Where is it any other, strategies in invasion whisper the continent, that finer rostrum of press, hearer and speaker divide only to redivide, com/posit each close thing until grouped to appear. A beat of a birdstaff, press pole upon pole, territory aright all along terrestory.

Softwood, presswood, allowed raise no deadly ash but upright powder the hills' wells and stools, followed but at none of the heath's answers. Tree beyond tree was never tree before but it could back onward, the press makes of every ecotone its tonal mat. Wallpoles open onto a field of poles where no row is easier than the spread it dates. Take out of time if the mass is not to have run out of difference.

Uniform locally expandible at maximal simplex (it being contiguous to press, tree after tree for in/nocence, knock on the same simple rate), multiplicavity of affixed points. The press-flow parts for no shelter but runs more paramount dilation, identifies with a loop, does not arch over in waiting curve. Shift each to each at side so centralizes so are many subgroups the centre with sides presses in, but tests to no point. All is meshed but nonwoven, the processional impoundments a non-frictional fill, forest inculcated tailings are fully softened strength.

The moor in a thin plate. Had it ever moved, is it moved over? Scaled on the same parasitic of shell to globe, it has, the press of trees is it coming, a difference of shock from a difference of not. Podsol was a seal not in favour of cover, a move-apparent in starved base. Trees are ungenerous ground by pressing for para/site, palisades open because the mesh is lean about slips for spacing, clearance into brushbox, the flex above ground slithering an arc of press.

The vacuum of takeover is a varium whither it cannot go but by which it stands up to ground having threaded the loop, a roof wheeling over catchment. Wave by wave folds the long hills by a wave afloat, uprightness being from the maltreated channel, a lateral feeding of soil. To profile across landscape surrenders its deeps to rolling fruit, degree of worth flattening out at wind table.

Heathrise of moonrise that much looser but with pouches of anglepress until a politics of alignment ascends the sky compatible in sufferance. All continuable parallels are standard, but never a purchase on content press to each hip, to each social take-up on the wing, or their flaps sewn open flounce backward onto cylinders of accession. The poles in ample press, a roof of theirs that covers ground and sky, press ground off, press sky off.

A rolling shoulder in place of base is "obscure enough". Some compression in the convention in order to take it down to others, but a general arrangement alongside, there to press. That habits excite serially in simply entering edge but by too many for any incision: as trees are known to stand. No brushes slot though flexibles corrode, neither are tops insular. The reclamation is by rowing out to each extra round until the incompletion's equal, no interpole nor any polarity in such shallow space. The press would not intensify, assumes but cover.

But is interior in as much as it traverses a world circling away, in long bands surrounded by shade to cover not curve. It has the absorption to impose, that is, impole, in not having to exist to principles already in shape. The lift flattens out rift at the edges spread where all such have ties, the additive common to the level being agreed to. No lifting but as ranks being let in, to extrapolate in college the pivots on naturalism, that secondary openness whose healing over within the space of a cultural incision reads across the knife along the trees' own axiate. A stance ever wider if trees were at every point of it, slow intricate winding because air and ground had not previously been there intimate. Therefore no spiral, no overlap, never underswaying at top though staggered at root.

Thrust without extraction, the press is not interaction. The earth lying out has no reserve against such sequence, is but a reserve tempered by what fares in the scar's decline, a surface pressed for to the relief of any image thrown up from underneath. The wood is steepening its kept-wood, widening its shaws, will press until the planet abates.

Conifers neither climbers nor runners press, only the exact pitched spire is to press absolute, each rod will turn about the sky until cover finds lateral consent. Whatever opening, whatever repetition, diverging road or violable spacing, it is written under the roof, this pressing of a level neither surface nor ground. Cover doesn't struggle by the root but the matter of wood is to suspend roots under its boughs. When cover hangs by the root its only tautness is the press. Carried on the shoulder but above the head, character of a layer there as not to ascribe, shade above mark. To a scribe above marked, but pressed open line across folded leaf.

No press will muster an unhygienic house. Recovery when it comes as a new danger hangs out its lure under a cover which thick-armed with the house suspends the house even while the matter of building is shed to reset surface. It is clearing as no press will. But how the branches push only to raise, erase, better of ground, clear types of press.

4 PEER WOODS

A likelihood of accident in the planted works not finishing on dangerous ground. But strikes barbarity the more loosely as to neighbourhoods peer, a branch beaten off gives sight to a parity no more winding than widening, hood up hood, wood up works. Way above for peering but between as taken, here it is a ramification of light, a beneception finally horizontal to nonopponent gaps, slender in stops with tricks on furtherance, may filter without turning cover. A glint along intervariate paths, half untwisted, trans hipped branches between guide behalf arches. Not peerless but light below canopy.

Peer drawn, for soon the tables roam, with bolder sweep along its branch table. With sweeping larch quality circles over domes of ladder, creeping rings. Calm oscillant, exploited of accident pitched at growth. Splinters are drawn to a ride arch, specked too linked but of myriad fascinations the glance fills every move though circum-sparse, in laps/e between searches and overhang, see if come, a bright slash of spars. Sighted space, lots look.

Cover erased out stretches, it arch-raced above ground, loose bound fast scaling, an allometry of light into branch decoy. With so much so much sees. From ground a spectrum of trees circling the arch where the verticals flaw a loft a look, in misapplied constancy a population of shapes but no impossible object imbues a rootedly abstract call, but in the air seeing where to go broadens the horizontal axis, not passing without peering. The need is constant awareness, to merit tangle, upon this it peers well.

Churnal leaves, the sacred hoop wide in daylight, starlight discs about the tree, with a tethering post it is a diameter of light. Curdled edging / uncurdled shore. Leaning the stem, see over centre to penetrable shelter: arch from peer, veers equal piers, a converse got above ground sees as if by open root. Summer hauls arbours but bowers becalm when stripped, strips of light in that gaze woven, direct image sheaf, locally free off a nilradical. And local solutions wield global patchings at length. The inverted tree is a spinal tree, arch on end between the reversible tree, dilates in the table's hollow, admits the tenderest tree amid peers.

The forest is the peering its like is, where the peers share between nature and scene, and blocks are as much unopposed as bad cuts are a law of area. Bark is a unit of tone but the glare angle is a radiance that had not reckoned on the covering look, the adjustment to canopy with its equal appearing intervals, the across-filter pattern that keeps to the horizontal path. There is no training here, but root and branch are for eyes alone. In that fall the space is open but ground rises.

The fall is a spear to oaks, scaffolding not impaired where leaf-dropping is a gentle anaesthetic. Sluggishly cleared to rigid room. Far from overthrown but stopped in its tracks with an efficiency thrown to the seen. Galleries and sinuses, the sun-invalidated leaf litter penetrable from every side, most radiant over gaps it was only every stripping, a peer's desire for traversal. Continuous droppings of freight, the continuals between. All trees have one or the other gymno-variant, either hardness or neatness. Ground is subsequent to cover looked off branches, the sudden paralysis which startles an access of community, not awaiting but overshooting the return to original acceleration, a cycle stolen but heeded in its sight. Such a future is nature frozen but naturally assertive where its expectancy was so traduced, every attractive thing extra peers into its anchor of arousal, that shelter-anger will clip to a traditionally dropped culture, hunger again periodical with figures.

The wood is not needful engineering but props to appearance, set to iterative arrays the inclusion of rays. Its uniform sloughed off in amounting site is but the carry-indication: it cannot spy on pores or along shelves of soil, is not a sleep interposed as energy but a loose piling source on the thinnest check of perspective, a filament unburied but among re-latents to confirm. A repose interstitial but closed into a group more helped off by mutations of light than naked. Such mutabilities put cultural manifestations of forest between us as if not yet exposed forward (and nature strips here), but the fenestration of whatever turn.

Synthetic variables as thrust up to cover, to be stripped or fletched, racked into sight. Comparison is bared with basis, nurture, position, limb. Limbs of seeing collect limbs undergoing, what will reveal, what will join it well, a cross-rewarding so numerous the incentive forks. Compounding figures, variable pressure-gaze on woodland. But were not the trees our equals we would have no students of the elevation. It hangs upon our gaze, as cover it will not fall over us but is lifted up on each generation's rota, the branch endings. Leaves not only opened out but throughout. With sight and ground as with root and arch, but cleaned out. All from cover to be over.

Thus a decreasingly filtered family swings above the cracking box of winter, as much for light, as though sight. Arches redundant to their caps, no indirect binding. Peers at what lean neighbours must be recording, animating in gaps, staying on across the reflex. Being switched off is so visibly the time for those that love you to get among you, sweet are your dry hollows, your combed staves, a concordance for the frequency of either root or cover.

Drawn through eloquent lists. Culture in the size of you, the skill of you upright. Co-kernel, co-appearance, branch and store, between all you have not hidden us, equal peers.

www.ingramcontent.com/pod-product-compliance
Lightning Source LLC
Chambersburg PA
CBHW022018160426
43197CB00007B/476
* 9 7 8 1 8 4 8 6 1 5 5 8 8 *